Evaluation-Based Leadership

SUNY Series in Educational Leadership
Daniel Duke, Editor

Evaluation-Based Leadership

School Administration in
Contemporary Perspective

Naftaly S. Glasman

State University of New York Press

Published by
State University of New York Press, Albany

Printed in the United States of America

For information, address State University of New York Press,
State University Plaza, Albany, N.Y., 12246

Library of Congress Cataloging-in-Publication Data

Glasman, Naftaly S., 1938–
    Evaluation-based leadership.

    (SUNY series in educational leadership)
    Bibliography: p. 173
    Includes index.
    1. School management and organization.
2. Leadership—Evaluation.   I. Title.   II. Series.
LB2805.L53   1986   371.2   85-31714
ISBN 0-88706-303-9
ISBN 0-88706-304-7 (pbk.)

10 9 8 7 6 5 4 3 2 1

To Lynne with love

Contents

Tables   xi

Figures   xiii

Preface   xv

Introduction   1

    School Leadership, 1
    Evaluation, 1
    Practical Issues for Principals, 2
    The School Leader as Evaluator, 3

Part I. Recent Demands for Evaluation   7

    1. The Increasing Focus on Evaluation in Education   9

        Past and Present Definitions, 9
        The Problem of Subjectivity, 11
        Current Models, 15

    2. Evaluation as a Political Value   19

        Politically Driven Policies, 19
        Awareness of Conflicts over Educational Values, 21
        Demands for Accountability, 23
        Some Observations, 26

3. Evaluation as a Destabilizing Force   27

    Evaluation and Organization, 27
    Control through Finance, 28
    A Multilevel Administration of Education, 30

4. The School District's Response   33

    Policy Changes, 34
    Structural Changes, 35
    Changes in Management and Decision-making Patterns,
      36
    Internal or External Institutionalization of Evaluation?, 38

5. Evaluation and Principals: A New Relationship   43

    Common Roots, 43
    Evaluation in Education Today, 44
    The Inevitability of a New Relationship, 46

Part II. *The School Principal's Response*   51

6. Linking the School Principal to Student Achievement:
   A Review of the Literature   53

    Ambiguities, 53
    Research on High-Performance Schools, 55
    The Question of How Principals Use Student,
      Achievement Data, 57

7. Introduction to a Statewide Study of
   Elementary School Principals   61

    Exploratory Field Data, 61
    Exploratory Review of the Literature, 62
    Sample of Principals Surveyed, 65
    Limitations of the Study, 69

8. School Leadership and Instructional Objectives   71

    Questions, 71
    Responses, 74
    Analysis, 76

9. School Leadership and Program Evaluation   83

    Questions, 83
    Responses, 86
    Analysis, 90

10. School Leadership and Interaction with Teachers   95

    Questions, 95
    Responses, 97
    Analysis, 99

11. School Leadership and Student
    Achievement Problems   105

    Questions, 105
    Responses, 108
    Analysis, 109

12. Student Achievement Data as an Administrative
    Resource: A Summary   113

    Commitment to Improving Student Achievement,
      113
    Control over the Use of Student Achievement Data,
      114
    Use of Student Achievement Data in Evaluation,
      115
    Effectiveness and Accountability, 116
    The Specific Issue of Principals' Accountability,
      117
    Direct Involvement with Achievement Problems,
      118
    Summary, 119

Part III. Critical Needs as Principals Perceive Them   121

13. Evaluation in Leadership Tasks: Molitor   123

    Awareness of the Concept, 123
    The Concept from the Principal's Perspective, 125
    Results, 126

14. Evaluation and Decisions: Gally 133

  Purpose and Method, 133
  Results, 135
  Comments, 138

15. Evaluation and Decisions: Lear 141

  Purpose and Method, 141
  Results, 143
  Comments, 147

16. The Judgmental Component 153

  A Letter to Former Students, 153
  Respondents and Responses, 157
  Analysis, 158

Part IV. Conclusion 161

17. Integrating the Facts 163

  Living with Demands for Accountability, 163
  Living with Daily Evaluation, 164

18. Further Study 169

  The Focus on Judgment, 169
  Evaluation Behavior, 170
  Principals' Orientation toward Evaluation, 171
  Concluding Remarks, 172

Bibliography 173

Index 193

Tables

7.1. Number of Schools in a California Elementary School District   67

7.2. Elementary School Principals' Responses on Sex, Age, and Years in Office   69

8.1. Responses of Principals to Questions Concerning Instructional Objectives   75

8.2. Significant Differences between Mean Responses of Principals to Questions 2, 3, and 4   80

8.3. Differences between Mean Responses of Principals to Four Groups of Questions   81

9.1. Responses of Principals to Questions Concerning the Use of Student Achievement Data in Program Evaluation   88–89

9.2. Interitem Correlations of Responses by 174 "Most Effective" Principals to Questions Concerning the Use of Student Achievement Data in Program Evaluation   91

9.3. Interitem Correlations of Responses by 97 "Least Effective" Principals to Questions Concerning the Use of Student Achievement Data in Program Evaluation   92

9.4. Differences between Mean Responses of Principals to Questions 7, 2, 5, and 1   93

10.1. Responses of Principals to Questions Concerning the Use of Student Achievement Data in Interactions with Teachers   98

10.2. Interitem Correlations of Responses by 174 "Most Effective" Principals to Questions Concerning the Use of Student Achievement Data in Interactions with Teachers   101

10.3. Interitem Correlations of Responses by 97 "Least Effective" Principals to Questions Concerning the Use of Student Achievement Data in Interactions with Teachers   102

11.1. Principals' Experience with Low Performance Scores   108

13.1. Time Principals Spend in Evaluation Activities   128–130

14.1. Attributes of Various Administrative Activities   136

14.2. Attributes of Activities Ending with Observed Decisions   138

15.1. Duration and Percent Distribution of Observed Activities by Type of Decision and Evaluation Component   145

15.2. Percent Distribution of Nine Evaluation Components in Four Types of Decisions   148

Figures

8.1. Differences Between Mean Responses on Groups of
      Questions in Principals' Group No. 1   78

8.2. Differences Between Mean Responses on Groups of
      Questions in Principals' Group No. 2   79

Preface

This book discusses the relationship between school leadership and evaluation. Leadership shapes events; evaluation facilitates change. Calls have been abundant in recent years for more effective leadership and for more useful evaluation.

Evaluation-based Leadership sees evaluation as one crucial component of leadership and focuses primarily on its use at the school level. In examining what principals think and do, it hopes to provide a more accurate picture of school leadership and to ultimately promote greater competency in that role.

To portray school leadership from this perspective is to pay respect to recent developments in American society which have called for more evaluation in education. This book suggests that the principalship may now be not only theoretically grounded in evaluation — as it has always been — but also driven by the new demands for higher educational quality.

This book replicates no other work. Although it contributes to the analysis of education, it is not a textbook on educational evaluation. Although it touches upon elements of pedagogy, supervision, management, and politics, it is not a treatise on effective school leadership (e.g., Morris et al. 1981; Duke 1982, 1984; Firestone and Wilson 1983; Iannaccone and Jamgochian 1985; Russel and Mazzarella 1985). And although it searches for creativity, wisdom, democratic attitudes, and the promotion of self-esteem in followers, it is not a survey of leadership in outstanding organizations (e.g., Deal and Kennedy 1982; Peters and Waterman 1982; Kantor 1983; and Kakabodes and Parker 1984). It is rather an extended focus on one particular element of school leadership today.

Acknowledgments

Many of my students and several of my colleagues have helped me sort out the issues of evaluation and leadership. Daniel Duke, Lois Patton, and five anonymous reviewers helped me improve earlier drafts. Barbara Hamill, Channing Hillway, and Patricia Skehan helped me preserve the fundamentals of the English language. I am grateful to them all.

The University of California, Santa Barbara, granted me time to write, and Beit Berl College in Israel provided me with a place to write. I appreciate their efforts.

My children, Ilan, Oren, and Mia, have inspired me on many a dawn and on many a sunset. My wife Lynne has contributed numerous ideas to this book. She has also helped me adjust to the recent loss of my parents; may their memory be blessed. I am fortunate to have such a family.

Introduction

School Leadership

The ability to lead depends upon the ability to understand one's own desires and the desires of other people. A leader is able to perceive what others want, which desires they pursue, and — at least in general terms — how they realize those desires. As a leader, therefore, the school principal must address both his or her own wants and those of the many individuals associated with the school. Some of those people learn, teach, counsel, or administer in the school building. Others — such as parents, school district office personnel, and educational policymakers and lawmakers — may work outside the school but still have a stake in what happens there. All these people may express their desires in a law, a formal policy, a formal decision, in tradition, or by less formal means. Some desires may be based heavily on objective realities; others, entirely on personal values. In dealing with all these demands, the principal sometimes influences how events unfold and sometimes reacts to developments. In other words, he or she is both before and alongside others.

Evaluation

Evaluation is the natural mental process by which people contemplate an object and eventually judge its worth for some purpose. If the person continues to be preoccupied with the object, his or her evaluation may eventually change. If it does not change, we say that the person has formed an "opinion." The evaluation of one object is often interrupted, consciously or unconsciously, when a person becomes aware of information about another object. The new object may or may not be directly related to the first object, but it does have some association with it.

Practical Issues for Principals

School principals, as leaders, have always had to deal both with their own demands and those of others inside and outside the school building. Inevitably, some of those demands have related to evaluations. Thus principals have had to decide what will be evaluated, for what purpose, how and when, and what will be done with the results of evaluations. As principals, they also have their own ideas about what should be evaluated. And they must determine which known wants are realized and how in order to shape the course of events in the school.

In recent years, the demands for evaluations by others outside the school have increased. The public, through its political representatives and with the aid of educational law and policy, has imposed new evaluation responsibilities on school principals. These demands have in turn prompted individual teachers and organized groups of teachers within schools to also call for evaluations of various kinds. Thus the principal must not only engage in the normal evaluations associated with being a leader, but also must evaluate the new demands for more evaluations. A new set of objects is being forced onto the principal's attention, a set which presents new problems but which still has some relation to the old.

For principals, the new situation has posed new questions, the most obvious of which is how to integrate the new demands into their own natural engagement in evaluation. Should a new demand, for example, be met in a superficial way or in an in-depth way? How does one evaluate the evaluation wants of other people? Although the new desires claim to be valid, they have no absolute validity (see Kahneman and Tversky 1973). Nevertheless, those wants exist (see Glasman and Sell 1972), and must therefore be evaluated. In addition, principals must now attempt to determine the consequences of their evaluations of these demands. They must be prepared to encounter and tolerate disagreements about their decisions, disagreements that may be based on differences in values, interpretations, or even information (Thompson 1982).

The new situation has also posed leadership issues, the most obvious one being how to lead when two sets of demands oppose more than complement each other. How do principals determine which demands correspond with their own, and how do they place themselves in a position ahead of others so that they can influence the pursuit of those demands? For example, their superiors may call for evaluating on the basis of student achievement, but their subordinates may caution against it. Or their superiors may call for evaluation reports at a given time, but their subordinates may insist that evaluation is a long and continuous process and should not be based on student achievement data alone. Each group wants the principal to lead everyone in the direction it prefers.

The School Leader as Evaluator

Discussing evaluation in connection with school leadership is like attaching advisors to decisionmakers. Much has been written on the relationship between the two. It has been portrayed as complex, private, delicate, mutually beneficial, and even mutually dependent. Examples of this relationship include court counselors and kings, special assistants and holders of political offices, troubleshooters and public figures, and consultants and corporate executives. In recent times, the relationship between social science researchers and public policymakers has been added to the list. An insightful analysis of that relationship was recently offered by Lindblom (1984). His analysis has much to offer to those attempting to address the issue of evaluation and school leadership.

Lindblom cites and challenges some common tenets which govern the relationship of social science researchers and public policymakers. Of specific interest to him are those that focus on the work of researchers. One tenet is that researchers should be concerned with the interest of the whole society rather than with some segment of it (p.3). Another tenet is that they should view a policy as the policymaker sees it rather than as others see it, including those who are affected by the policy (p.5). The third tenet is that they should recommend courses of action to policymakers (p.5).

Lindblom dismisses all three tenets as wrong and offers opposites to each of them. First, he calls for "thoughtful partisanship": an acknowledgment that research is guided by "a selection of some among

other possible interests or values" and that the researchers' version of
the public interest is partisan (p. 15). He is against "selling" research by
proclaiming that it serves the public good. Lindblom's position is based
on the argument that no one knows what the public interest as a whole
really is. Knowledge can help form a commitment up to a point, but
beyond that point, there is nothing more to know that will expedite a
resolution of a conflict: a decision simply must be made (pp.8–9).

As to the second tenet, Lindblom believes in helping the ordinary
citizen and not only the policymaker, who supposedly serves the plea-
sure of some unified public (p.24). Lindblom dismisses the notion of
a uniform public belief (say, in the Constitution or in free enterprise)
because even accumulated research knowledge about such possible
uniformity creates diversity rather than agreement among researchers.
Nor does tradition prove that a uniformity of belief exists. The family,
the school, and religion transfer diversity, and that diversity is a product of indoctrination more than it is a product of truth (pp.26–30).
Lindblom calls for redirecting social science research to the needs of
the ordinary citizen, who in turn may redirect his own needs — may
engage in constructing his own volitions more than in trying to uncover
his or others' preferences (pp.30–35).

Lindblom is also against researchers recommending particular
courses of action. He would rather see research tailored to meet
various specific critical needs. For example, researchers might uncover
missing facts, analyze complex interconnections, challenge tentatively
reached conclusions, and checklist pertinent variables and possible
solutions to a problem (pp.36–38).

Part I of this volume shows that the increased visibility of evaluation has been expedited on the basis of a supposed concern for the
public good — that is, by "nonpartisan" techniques. However, these
techniques have served policymakers more than they have improved
educational quality. The resulting policies have not been based on solid
educational research but have been driven by the demands of an
increasing number of evaluation "specialists." Policymakers have used
the concern for evaluation, moreover, to increase their control over
local school districts, largely by tying evaluation to funding. As a
result, districts have had to deal more and more with external demands
and have had less time to deal with internal problems.

Part II discusses how school leaders have responded to this situation. The surveys of principals' beliefs presented in these chapters show

that, among other things, principals are much clearer about what the district wants them to do than what they themselves would like to do and can do. Moreover, although they try to satisfy the new demands, they are largely uncertain about the actual effects of evaluation on student achievement. In short, principals have had to respond in an ambivalent manner: sometimes obeying external mandates, and sometimes doing what they think is best. Making these decisions is in itself an evaluation process.

Part III then attempts to discover what principals themselves perceive as critical needs — in other words, the "partisan" rather than the "nonpartisan" viewpoint. These chapters discuss various studies which have attempted to determine principals' perceptions of school problems, how much they engage in evaluation, and how they render judgments as they respond to various problems. Special attention is given to the judgmental component of the principals' decision-making process. These studies lead to the conclusion that, as Lindblom maintains, effective decisions have to be partisan in nature and must be associated with personal attempts to meet self-perceived critical needs.

Part I

Recent Demands for Evaluation

In recent years, evaluation of education has been practiced extensively at federal, state, county, and school district levels, as well as in schools and in classrooms. Millions of evaluations are expressed orally every day. Probably thousands of evaluation reports are written every day.

The process of evaluation has also been studied extensively. Publications on this subject are probably multiplying by the month. Evaluation is studied from a variety of approaches, including measurement, learning, curriculum, instruction, counseling, administration, organizations, values, and politics. At least a dozen academic disciplines have had an interest in this topic, among them psychology, sociology, economics, political science, history, anthropology, philosophy, mathematics, and computer science. Most writings about evaluation are selective and intentional, and this volume is no exception. Part I, which outlines recent developments concerning evaluation of education, is selective in the sense that it discusses only those aspects which are deemed highly pertinent to school leaders. It is intentional in the sense that it emphasizes the need for school leaders and students of school leadership to recognize the impact of these developments on the role of school principal.

Chapter *1*

The Increasing Focus on Evaluation in Education

Past and Present Definitions

The history of evaluation in education began before the turn of the century. Most of the recorded accounts appear to be relatively brief and intentional. In volume after volume on this topic, one can detect no more than a few dozen pages of history. These pages are usually followed by as many as a few hundred pages in which a "new" model of evaluation is presented.

These brief historical accounts reveal three seemingly distinct periods. The first lasted until the 1930s, the second until the 1960s, and the third seems to be presently going on. In each of these periods, expansion rather than replacement of the "old" seems to characterize the succession of ideas.

Evaluation in education was first seen as measurement. The focus was on measuring the intelligence level of a child or a child's ability to learn a particular subject. Most histories imply a close association between evaluation as measurement and the scientific paradigm of inquiry prevalent in the early part of the twentieth century. This paradigm was viewed at the time as a success story. It was widely and extensively used in the physical and life sciences and was eagerly legitimized as a mode of inquiry in the behavioral and social sciences. When the scientific movement granted a somewhat tentative approval to psychology and a more hesitant green light to education, those two disciplines also began to employ the scientific paradigm. Educational measurement won several adherents during World War I.

9

The early conception of educational measurement had three fundamental characteristics: it focused on differences among individuals, it dealt with almost nothing else, and it employed standardized measures of individual differences. While psychology measured a wide range of subjects, education measured only a given subject matter content which was taught and learned in schools. Tests were constructed to measure differences among individual learners. Excluded were all other types of possible differences which may be found in education and in schools, such as those among textbooks, lessons, teachers, principals, boards, ideologies, and finances. No assessment was made of curricula. Rather, norms were set for differences among learners. These norms were associated with a given age of a child or with a given placement of a child at a given grade level. A child's performance was measured against the performance of others in his class or age group.

The tasks of educational evaluation expanded in the late 1930s and in the 1940s. Tyler (1950) helped broaden the definition to include the determination of the extent to which educational objectives are being realized. This definition implied that the purpose of evaluation was to improve school curricula. Tyler introduced a set of procedures which he believed would accomplish this purpose. He conceived of a pool of possible educational objectives that would be derived from the opinions of curriculum experts. He suggested that the objectives be examined from three perspectives: philosophical (the importance of the objectives), psychological (the influence of the objectives on students), and experiential (how the objectives could be achieved). Tyler conceived of a content area as an expected set of student behaviors that would meet the educational objectives that had survived the above examination. He suggested that specific learning situations be identified in which students could exhibit the behaviors stipulated by each objective. He also suggested that tests be constructed with the highest degrees of reliability and validity to examine whether the objectives would be achieved. On the basis of the test results, areas of strength and weakness in the curricula would be identified, examined, and modified as necessary.

The definition of evaluation in education was further expanded during the 1960s to include its relationship to decision making. Several versions of how this definition would operate are found in the literature. The common focus was on providing information to decisionmakers (e.g., Cronbach 1963; Stufflebeam 1966; Provus 1967; Alkin 1969).

One group of individuals (Stufflebeam et al. 1971) proposed an all-inclusive focus and defined evaluation as the process of "delineating, obtaining, and providing useful information for judging decision alternatives" (p.40). The authors provided extensive rationales for each of the terms used in the definition.

By the 1970s, evaluation in education had come to include all of its earlier meanings. It was the measurement of individual differences in relation to the achievement of curricular objectives, and its function was to provide information to decisionmakers. This broadened definition also acknowledged that decisions concerning evaluations require judgment. In the 1970s, therefore, evaluation was seen as the process of collecting information and judging its worth or merit (e.g., Scriven 1967; Stake 1967; Glass 1969; Stufflebeam 1974a; Eisner 1979; House 1980; Guba and Lincoln 1981). This acknowledgment paved the way for later demands for systematic evaluation (House 1974; Cronbach et al. 1980).

The Problem of Subjectivity

For those who practice evaluation, the acknowledgement of subjectivity is a necessity. For students of evaluation, subjectivity has been a field of study and has been detected and exposed in several areas (Glasman 1979a).

The original definition of evaluation as measurement of individual differences centered on the performance of students, which was deemed the ultimate product of learning. This definition has had the longest history of all such definitions. It was finally acknowledged, however, that absolute standards of student performance simply do not exist. First, standards vary with the content and difficulty of the subject matter. Second, the act of setting performance standards, whether on the basis of a theory or the consensus of experts, involves some judgment. A theory of education is derived from a theory of prerequisites, which cannot be defined with absolute clarity. A consensus is produced when judges disagree.

The acknowledgement that absolute standards of student performance do not exist paved the way for the movement away from norm-referenced standards and toward standards based on certain criteria. (Norm-referenced tests use measures which determine a student's standing relative to a reference group to which the student belongs [age, grade]. Criterion-referenced tests use measures which determine a student's standing relative to a level of performance which the student is expected to achieve.) At first, criterion-referenced scores were supposed to indicate student performance relative to an achievement criterion (Glaser and Klaus 1962), but it turned out that achievement criteria were based on test results which employed grading categories that were chosen in a totally subjective manner (Glass 1977).

Subjective judgment was employed in evaluating teacher performance to an even greater extent than it was in evaluating student performance (Glasman 1979a). Here, too, the standards were not based on norms. But they also suffered from a lack of clarity about the relationship between student performance and teacher behavior (Flanders and Simon 1969; Bidwell 1973; Shavelson and Dempsy-Atwood 1976; Millman 1981). This relationship was viewed in two ways. One view saw teacher performance as a function of student performance; the other view recognized no such dependence. In the former, domain-referenced tests were employed to establish standards of teacher performance. Students were examined on a specific topic within a specific subject matter which the teacher taught. The students' scores were used to evaluate the performance of the teacher. But subjective judgement was used not only in testing student performance, but also when one domain was weighed in comparison to another in the performance of teachers. Even when no connection was made between teachers and student performance, several problems existed with the very definition of effective teaching and its criteria (Powell and Beard 1984).

Making evaluations in any domain in education involves making subjective judgments, from setting a goal to selecting and using evaluation data. The elements of subjectivity in program evaluation have been studied extensively. In the 1970s, concerted efforts were made to neutralize this subjectivity. For example, it was suggested that the evaluator should begin working without knowing the stated goals of the program that was being evaluated (Scriven 1973). It was also suggested that evaluators themselves be viewed as an integral part of the measurement instrument and that they record all of the thoughts which they have while they observe, seek data, and evelute (Eisner 1975).

These attempts tried to eliminate subjectivity in the evaluator. But they did not and could not eliminate the subjectivity of those who supplied the evaluation data and of those whose efforts were being evaluated. School district psychologists, for example, may wish or may be told to "produce" large or small numbers of students of a certain "type" for particular specialized programs. When they do so, they employ subjective judgments which cannot be neutralized effectively later when these programs are evaluated. When they need to produce more "gifted" students to qualify for additional funding, they choose a test which is standardized on a slightly and positively skewed normative population because of the lower mean. When they need to produce fewer "less educable" students so as to permit the district to save money by mainstreaming these students, they choose a given available test and tolerate a relatively low score loss.

After the 1970s, sincere and useful attempts were made to neutralize some of the elements of subjectivity in educational evaluation, most of them with the inherent and publicized intention of making the expanded version of evaluation in education more systematic and therefore more acceptable. One set of attempts was designed to improve the methodology of evaluation; a second, to improve how it is used; and a third, to improve its standards. All three sets pertain, primarily, to evaluation of educational programs.

In methodology, improvements occurred in both quantitative and qualitative approaches. Berk (1981) focused on the quantitative paradigm, whose attributes include views which are positivistic, hypothetico-deductive, particularistic, and outcome oriented. Specific improvements in the methodology are summarized by various authors in Berk's volume. They include clarification of terminology, synthesis of research, translation of research results into forms which are useful to evaluators, and a somewhat sharper focus on major issues in educational evaluation. Patton (1980) focused on the qualitative paradigm, which relies on qualitative data, holistic analysis, and detailed descriptions derived from close contacts with the targets of study. This paradigm employs techniques of in-depth, open-ended interviews and personal observations. Improvements have included specifying the choices associated with design and improved data collection and analysis techniques. The choices themselves have been grounded in the perspective that evaluation is active, reactive, and adaptive with respect to particular situations.

The use of evaluation was forcefully developed, practiced, and examined after the mid-1970s. Patton (1978) developed a "utilization-focused" approach to evaluation by conceiving of it as necessarily "political" in nature because it possesses the power to influence decisionmakers. He argued that the power of evaluation varies with the degree to which its findings reduce uncertainty for given decisionmakers (p. 50). Patton's approach does several things. It identifies and classifies relevant decisionmakers and those who use evaluation information. It identifies relevant evaluation questions. It selects evaluation methods which generate useful information. It encourages decisionmakers and evaluation information users to participate, along with evaluators, in data analysis and interpretation. Finally, it provides for negotiation and cooperation between evaluators and others involved in evaluation dissemination (pp. 284–289).

Alkin, Daillak, and White (1979) complemented Patton's work by classifying the factors which they believe influence how evaluation information is used by decisionmakers. On the basis of several case studies, they identified eight categories of factors (see Alkin, Daillak, and White, chapter 9 and appendix 2). Category 1 is preexisting evaluation bounds. It includes school community conditions, the mandated bounds of the evaluation, fiscal constraints, and other nonnegotiable requirements. Category 2 is the orientation of evaluation users. It includes concerns about the program which is evaluated, expectations for the evaluation, and preferred forms of evaluation information. Category 3 is the approach of the evaluator. It includes the evaluator's use of formal evaluation model, research and analysis considerations, choice of role, the nature of user involvement, the manner of dealing with mandated tasks of evaluation, rapport, and the evaluator's manner of facilitating and stimulating the use of information. Category 4 is the credibility of the evaluator and includes specificity and changeability. Category 5 focuses on organizational factors, including interrelationships between individual schools and the district office, other evaluation information sources, student views, and costs and rewards. Category 6 focuses on extraorganizational factors, including the influence of communities and government agencies. The last two categories are evaluation information content and reporting, and administrator style. The former covers substance, format, and information dialogue. The latter covers administrative and organizational skills, and initiative.

The practicality of evaluation was of particular concern during the late 1970s with regard to the use of educational program evaluation, and was closely connected with the earlier notion of the influence which evaluation findings had on decisionmakers (Tuckman 1979; Patton 1982). Specific suggestions were offered as to how practicality may be conceived, developed, practiced, and assessed.

The third significant development in the practice and study of evaluation since the late 1970s included attempts to improve its standards. The most comprehensive attempt was published by the Joint Committee on Standards for Educational Evaluation (1981). This publication identifies and elucidates thirty separate standards, each of which is explained and clarified through a commentary. Each commentary includes an overview of the purpose of the standard, guidelines for its application, common pitfalls associated with the application, warnings against overzealousness in implementing the standard, and an illustration of the standard's application. The overall reported rationale for the establishment of the standards is that evaluation is inevitable. Some standards will therefore promote sound evaluation and improve education. The standards, in essence, provide advice for dealing with criteria by which to judge educational programs, projects, and materials.

The list of thirty standards is grouped into four categories — utility, feasibility, propriety, and accuracy standards. Utility standards include those for audience identification, evaluator credibility, information scope and selection, valuational interpretation, report clarity, report dissemination, report timeliness, and evaluation impact. Feasibility standards include those for practical procedures, political viability, and cost effectiveness. Propriety standards include those for formal obligation, conflict of interest, full and frank disclosure, public's right to know, rights of human subjects, human interactions, balanced reporting, and fiscal responsibility. Accuracy standards include those for object identification, context analysis, described purposes and procedures, defensible information sources, valid measurement, reliable measurement, systematic data control, analysis of quantitative information, analysis of qualitative information, justified conclusions, and objective reporting.

Current Models

Over the years, several models have been developed for evaluation in education, most of which have evolved from the practice of evaluation as much as they have guided that practice. Their usefulness has been tested by both experience and research. Nevo (1983) summarizes them for nonspecialists and a selected overview and interpretation of that summary is presented below. The overview is grounded in a concern for assumptions about what evaluation is, how it is done, and who does it.

The "what" question focuses on the definition of evaluation, its functions, its objects, the information which is collected, and the criteria for judging it. A currently acceptable definition of evaluation in education is that it is a systematic description of educational objects and an assessment of their worth or merit. A currently acceptable list of evaluation functions includes improvement ("formative" evaluation), selection and accountability ("summative" evaluation), motivation and gain of public support ("psychological and sociopolitical" evaluation), and the exercise of authority ("administrative" evaluation). The last-mentioned is the newest function which has been recognized (Dornbusch and Scott 1975; Johnson and Glasman 1983). There are numerous objects of evaluation and types of evaluation information. Typical and broadly conceived objects include students, personnel, curricula, materials, buildings, finances, programs, and institutions. Typical and broadly conceived information types include goals, plans, plan implementations, and outcomes. The merit of described objects may be judged according to whether they achieve their goal, respond to client needs, and meet agreed-upon standards.

The "how" question entails the process of conducting the evaluation and the use of inquiry methods. The process of evaluation, broadly conceived, involves focusing on a problem, collecting and analyzing relevant empirical data, and communicating the findings of the investigation. The problem may be studied with the use of experimental designs, quasi-experimental designs, naturalistic methods, case study methods, jury trials, and journalistic methods. Each method of inquiry has its own strengths and weaknesses. Which method is used depends on the specific problem and its circumstances.

The "who" question entails two interrelated concerns: the identity of the client(s) and the identity of the evaluator(s). The literature on evaluation prefers to asssume that the client and the evaluator are two different persons or groups of persons. Frequently mentioned clients are decisionmakers, policy-shaping communities, and those who may be effected by an evaluation. Evaluator types are frequently divided into two groups: for example, internal (in-house) and external (outside) evaluators, and professional (trained) and amateur evaluators. Professional evaluators are usually competent in educational measurement and understand the contextual parameters of evaluation. They must also have personal attributes such as integrity, trustworthiness, objectivity, and personability.

The development of the large variety of evaluation models has been closely related to the increasing number of actual evaluations conducted over the years, as well as to the increasing number of scholarly treatments of those evaluations. Evaluation in education has become a specialty in terms of both practice and scholarly inquiry. The more evaluation has been systematized, the more it has gained acceptance. Evaluation models have been offered in the name of improving education and learning in schools. The fact that the desired improvement itself lacks clarity has bothered only few evaluation scholars and practitioners. Evaluation specialists have been busy collecting knowledge about evaluation in order to form a commitment to the evaluation process.

Evaluation as a specialty in education is a twentieth century phenomenon. Its increased visibility in recent years is largely the result of needs which evaluation practitioners and scholars have perceived and promoted. This increase during the last decade and a half has had other causes as well, particularly those associated with the intensification of the political demands for evaluation. These are addressed in the next chapter.

Chapter *2*

Evaluation as
a Political Value

Politically Driven Policies

The study of educational politics has become somewhat systematic only since the late 1950s (Scribner 1977; Wirt and Kirst 1982). Until that time, the myth had prevailed that education and politics do not mix. One focus in the study of educational politics in the past thirty-five years has been on educational policies. Three questions have been investigated: what the policies are, how they emerge, and what their influence is.

The most common definition of an educational policy has been rooted in the view that policies are embodiments of political values (Easton 1965). These political values may be material values (having to do with tangible resources, such as money) or symbolic values (having to do with ideologies, beliefs, and emotional needs, such as for status), and they originate in a source of stress somewhere in the society. This stress generates demands on the political system, as well as support for a response. The political system then responds by making policies that feed back values to the rest of society. Policies thus may be indicative of how the political system allocates material and symbolic values to individuals and groups.

Educational policies have come in the form of statutes, court decisions, ordinances, resolutions, executive orders, memoranda, referenda, and other less formal forms. Individuals and agencies involved in their articulation, enactment, and implementation have included voters, federal and state authorities, local lay and educational authorities, school site professionals, associations, businesses, industries, and others. They have had an impact on school finance, organization of education, school curricula, teaching, student graduation requirements, educational opportunities, and educational accountability.

There is little evidence that educational policymakers have searched for and used systematically collected educational data to depoliticize or at least neutralize the roots of their policies. Optimists believe that the link between research data and educational policies can be improved. Pessimists do not believe so.

Some optimists (Klitgard 1974; Light 1979) recommend that policy outcomes be measured by various methods and that alternative policies be compared. For example, policies should be measured by the changes that are initiated in schools as well as the effects such changes have on children. Evaluators should acknowledge the inexactness of their findings and any conflicting outcomes, and should also assess the value of their findings for various interest groups.

Other optimists (Cohen and Weiss 1977; Rein and White 1977; Immegart and Boyd 1979) suggest that research problems be identified as relevant or not relevant to known agendas of educational policy making. They argue that this identification will help redefine problems, multiply viewpoints, increase diversity in the treatment of evidence, demystify the technical aspects of research, create an effective coalition for action at the appropriate government level, provide an ideology that helps create coalitions, and manage dilemmas and trade-offs so as to provide arguments for the supremacy of some particular policy position.

Pessimists do not believe that improving research data nor increasing its relevance to policy making will solve two fundamental problems which plague the relationship between research and policy. Glass (1977) deals with the problem of researching the effects of a policy. He contends that, although researchers might imagine themselves discovering policy which is prescribed by organizational leaders for other members of the organization (top-down prescriptive policy), such a phenomenon in fact does not exist. It is simply impossible to predict which of several things works well in particular circumstances. Variance in the effects of a policy, according to Glass, is inexplicable in particular circumstances and cannot be measured and controlled. Policy analysis studies have not assumed that what produces an effect in schools is liable to be controlled by persons who are far from the essential link between the student's brain and a tutor. Iannaccone (1978) deals with the problem of the limitations of research methodologies. According to him, the error factor of the science of technology exacerbates value conflicts in society by increasing the disillusionment with education. This error factor refocuses the political conflicts upon the criterion purposes and goals of the society.

Awareness of Conflicts over Educational Values

It may be that the difference between the optimists and the pessimists is a matter of degree. Neither group would deny that the link between educational research data and educational policy making is at best very weak. Top-down prescriptive policies over the years have primarily embodied the material and symbolic values of society. One set of symbolic values has been rooted in public awareness of cleavages within the society about educational values themselves.

These conflicts have reflected tensions between the egalitarian desire to educate all children and the elitist desire of each family to ensure the best education for its own children. These tensions have never been completely resolved because the two desires are inherently contradictory. In theory, two fundamental situations may exist. When tensions are converted, through the political system, into material values or policies which satisfy dominant desires, the result has a significant influence on what is taught in public schools, how, and by whom. At those times, awareness of conflicts is low. However, when tensions are such that there is a need for the political system to allocate symbolic values, the political system does not respond in a way which satisfies everyone. At those times, awareness of conflicts is high. The last one hundred years can be divided into three successive periods which differed significantly from one another in the awareness of conflicts over educational values. Awareness was moderately high until about 1915, was relatively low between 1915 and the late 1950s, and has been extremely high since then (Glasman 1979b).

In the first period, lay persons were continuously and intensively involved in education to ensure that a given value position in a given locality was dominant. Lay school boards ran the day-to-day activities in the schools. They examined pupils, chose textbooks, and selected and certified teachers (Cubberly 1916). Value conflicts over educational issues were visible through partisan political controversies as state after state was involved in compulsory school legislation. The high public awareness of value conflicts in education was somewhat subsumed, however, within a large number of other political controversies. Local school board elections were held on dates when other municipal and state elections were held. Attempts to resolve educational conflicts were somewhat confined to board activities during its tenure. Thus, the awareness by the general public of value conflicts in education during that period was only moderately high.

The awareness of conflicting values between 1915 and the late 1950s declined as the intensity of conflicts over issues decreased. The mandate to run the schools shifted from local school boards to employed school administrators. Society agreed less over educational issues and more over the merit of science as a key to the resolution of conflicts in general. Local school boards, like other public agencies, were caught up by the evolution of the scientific ideology (Callahan 1962), particularly in the area of finance, where efficiency was demanded (Mort, Rensger, and Polley 1960). Issues such as what was taught in schools, how, and by whom were not deemed as important as the need by school districts to employ businesslike bookkeeping procedures. The authority of local school boards was weakened (Ziegler, Tucker, and Wilson 1977). Elections of board members were held separately from other municipal and state elections and by nonpartisan ballots. At the same time, the authority of district superintendents expanded, and the superintendency became more professionalized (Campbell, Corbally, and Ramseyer 1961). Conflicts over professionization issues between boards and superintendents (Lutz and Iannaccone 1978) were much more dominant than conflicts over what gets taught in schools, how, and by whom.

A gradual but significant increase in the awareness of conflicting values in education has occurred since the late 1950s. Social unrest has turned to lay dissatisfaction with schools. Schools have become focal points of political battles. The lay public, through its political representatives, has promoted an intensified use of scientific methods and technologies in evaluating education, even though this use turned out not to be highly relevant to educational policy making (Brickell 1976; Berk and Rossi 1977; Sroufe 1977). Differences between the values of science and the values of education became apparent when it was realized that a more intensified use of scientific measurement would not resolve fundamental value issues in education. Nonetheless, major state educational finance reforms occurred in the 1970s (Garms, Guthrie, and Pierce 1978; Guthrie 1980), and many other state reforms occurred in the early 1980s (United States Department of Education 1984) in areas such as textbooks, career ladders for teachers, performance-based pay for teachers, and graduation requirements for students.

Awareness of conflicts over educational values, then, has forced the political system to respond. But it has never done so in a completely satisfactory manner because a complete consensus over the values themselves has never been reached. Even when awareness of these conflicts was low, particularly when value differences about education were concealed behind an overwhelming and uniting ideology, the society forced the political system to respond.

Demands for Accountability

Over the years, political dynamics resulting from value conflicts over education have produced demands for accountability in education. These demands have been transformed through the political system into educational policies. There may be several ways to determine the nature, causes, and effects of government policies designed to cope with specific societal problems. One approach views policies as givens and studies their determinants; another views societal forces as givens and studies what policies they produce; a third views policies as givens and studies their effects; and a fourth views effects as givens and studies how they are promoted by policies (Nagel 1980). The influence of various institutions on the political system, including educational institutions, can also be studied (Dornhoff 1980).

The previous section in this chapter was rooted, in part, in Dornhoff's view of educational institutions as forces that influence the political system. It was also somewhat rooted in Nagel's first approach, which describes the need by the political system to respond to awareness of conflicts over educational issues. This section essentially adopts Nagel's second approach. It views the awareness of conflicts over educational values as given political forces and government demands for educational accountability as the policies which the political forces produce. Those demands are thus viewed here as one kind of response by the political system to tensions within the society at large.

At the most general level, which encompasses the whole history of demands for educational accountability, these demands convey the notion that schools and educators who operate them must be held responsible for what they do and answerable to the general public. Because demands for accountability have occurred in different historical contexts, they have also had various focuses — curriculum, instruction, teachers, administrators, student performance expectations, institutional responsiveness through lay participation, finances, and ideology.

Since the turn of the twentieth century, three fundamental criteria for educational accountability have been identified: efficiency, equality, and quality (Glasman 1983a). Each of these criteria was rooted in a specific set of value conflicts which existed at a given time in the society at large as well as in education in particular. All three criteria were handed to the schools from higher-level governments and produced a variety of uncertainties at the local level, particularly for school administrators. The effects of those accountability criteria are described later in this volume. A more detailed outline of the criteria themselves follows.

The *efficiency* criterion in the society as a whole appeared in the form of demands for considerating production-to-cost ratios. Early in the twentieth century, the United States Office of Education began to standardize accounting for schools. This effort emphasized technical efficiency and was a movement toward uniformity and specificity in school budgeting and accounting (James 1981). At the same time, needs were articulated (Taylor 1911) for finding the best way to work and for placing responsibility for this task on management. As a result, shifts occurred in the locus of the control of budgeting and accounting. In education, that control was vested in the local school superintendent and the local school board. A variety of production-to-cost ratio considerations developed (Barnard 1938), most notably focusing on efficiency measures of educational finance (Callahan 1962) and including financial allocations, financial expenditures, and financial monitoring and auditing.

Historical parallels have been suggested between the effects of demands for financial accountability in the society as a whole and those in education. Within education itself, parallels can be drawn between the effects of demands for fiscal accountability in education and those for student performance accountability in schools. For example, the early emphasis on measuring the attainment of educational objectives by student intelligence (Tyler 1950; Bloom et al. 1971) and the early efficiency measures of educational finance occurred at about the same time.

The *equality* criterion in the society as a whole appeared in the form of demands on government and business to provide members of disadvantaged populations with extended opportunities (Lipset 1963) or improved performance (Ryan 1981). The demands intensified in the 1950s and, in education, they have appeared to have many meanings (Kirp 1982, chapter 3). One demand has been for the equal provision of minimum levels of educational resources, services, and performance. (Coleman et al. 1966; Mosteller and Moynihan 1972). Essentially, the promotion of equal educational opportunities continues to be both a hope and a reflection of unresolved social issues outside the schools. The interrelationships between judicial decisions and political activities associated with the drive toward this equality continue to produce different meanings.

The *quality* criterion of educational accountability has become a central concern in recent years. Social and economic problems intensified in the 1970s. The identity of their causes and solution was unclear. Quality became, among other things, an economic and moral issue and turned, in part, into dissatisfaction with what the schools were doing. The public also became more aware of the actual decline in student achievement test scores. Demands for school quality turned into demands for school effectiveness. Of concern were the effects schools had upon achievement scores. First, the public demanded accurate information (such as test scores) about school performance (Wynne 1972). Then the calls became more specific. One such call was for technically sound, systematic, and objective proofs of student achievement, which is stipulated in terms of the initial abilities of the students and the conditions under which they study and which indicates different expectations for different characteristics of students (Alkin and Glasman 1975). In the 1980s, the calls were at the forefront of political debates. They produced an utmost sense of urgency because they shook the public's confidence in the public schools.

Some Observations

So far, this chapter has argued that educational policies in general are politically driven transmissions of values which are allocated in response to demands and with the help of supporting groups and individuals. It has also argued that educational policies are not influenced greatly by the data which educational research generates. Ironically, educational evaluation policies intensified without a corresponding intensification of research-based educational policies. It would seem that evaluation specialists were better at appearing to be nonpartisan than were educational researchers. The former group succeeded in selling their goods to policymakers, while the latter group did not. It is interesting in this regard that early evaluation literature carefully distinguishes between two kinds of people who are interested in the results of evaluation studies. One kind includes nonevaluators (laypeople); the other kind includes researchers. As it turned out, policymakers responded, at least in rhetoric, to the evaluators in a nonpartisan way: they accepted the intensification of evaluation policies in the interest of the public good.

Chapter *3*

Evaluation as a Destabilizing Force

Evaluation and Organization

Evaluation and organization are sometimes viewed as conflicting terms (Wildavsky 1972). Organization implies stability, while evaluation implies change. Organization focuses on relating activities to programs and clients. Evaluation focuses on relating activities to objectives, and in so doing may destabilize the relation between programs and clients. If an organization voluntarily takes on the task of self-evaluation, therefore, it risks self-destruction. If it is faced with externally mandated evaluation, it searches for ways to avoid self-destruction. It can avoid this problem more easily if it can pass on the responsibilities for evaluation to others.

A more systematized evaluation in education was first mandated at the federal level and soon thereafter at the state level. Federal and state organizations which dealt with education viewed the mandate to evaluate education, in part, as a mandate to evaluate themselves. During the late 1970s and early 1980s, federal and state educational leaders managed to preserve their organizations by passing on evaluation responsibilities to local school districts. They did so largely by allocating funds for evaluation. The mechanisms used by federal officials to allocate those funds were not exactly identical to those used by state officials, but the motive was the same: to preserve the organization by passing on responsibility and money to others. Political compromises at the federal and state levels expedited the articulation and enactment of evaluation-based funding legislation.

27

Federal education officials have never had genuine autonomy. They have been part of a political establishment which has called for educational innovations that have necessitated the allocation of federal funds and federal requirements for evaluation. The calls for dollars and for evaluation reflected, at most, partisan politics and, at least, the support for a policy. The federal organization responded to these calls in two ways. It provided grants-in-aid to state and local organizations and mandated that the use of the funds be evaluated. The responsibility for evaluation was delegated to state and local educational agencies. In this way, the federal organization succeeded in stabilizing its own environment despite the high rates of change at the state and local levels (Glasman 1983a). The established principle was that state government was legally responsible for public education and that local school districts were arms of the state. This principle was used by the federal organization to justify its demands for evaluation despite concerns which were raised by local education agencies (Rutherford and Hoffman 1981).

Once the pressure was off the federal organization, it shifted to the state level. The intensified calls for educational accountability and reform in the early 1980s accentuated the central role of state government. State education officials found themselves in predicaments similar to those in which federal officials had earlier found themselves; the difference was that state officials were unable to delegate all their responsibilities for evaluation to local officials (Glasman 1982). State leaders used evaluation selectively to legitimize existing policies. They even publicized evaluation results selectively. Evaluation was used at the state level as an instrument for supporting policy. State-mandated, evaluation-based funding multiplied in quantity, scope and depth, particularly following a brief financial retrenchment period which ended when finances for education became a political necessity and therefore more abundant.

Control through Finance

Even before this increase in mandate concerning evaluation, historical parallels had existed between educational evaluation and educational finance in terms of sources, purposes, and forms (Johnson 1980). The link between the two has intensified through evaluation-based fiscal legislation in recent years (Glasman 1979b, 1983a). The structure of control within the educational system was also significantly affected. Essentially, new fiscal legislation reflected demands for quality and effectiveness. Evaluation was used as a political resource designed to influence the allocation and management of public funds earmarked for education. Funding decisions became closely linked to the nature and scope of the assessment of individual school districts and schools which were receiving the funds. Most funds were allocated in the form of categorical rather than general aid to ensure that they would be used as much as possible in accordance with the legislation.

In thus allocating funds, the grantor — the higher level of government — was trying to maintain control over the grantee — the lower level of government — in matters involving preferences, the relative price of goods, and income (Tsang and Levin 1983). The grantee's preferences could be altered if the grantor focused on an educational goal and legislated its achievement. The relative price of goods could be altered if the grantor paid the full cost or part of the cost of implementing the legislation. Income could be altered if the grantor augmented it.

At least two kinds of situations have arisen in this allocation of funds. In one, the grantee agency has used the money for the grant's intended purpose, sometimes providing additional funds for the same purpose from its own resources. In this situation, the grantor has had extensive control. The second situation is when the grantee agency has not used all the grant for its intended purpose but has used some of it to reduce the level of its own funds previously earmarked for the given purpose, thereby freeing funds for other purposes or reducing income from other sources such as local taxation. In this situation, the grantor has not had complete control. Tsang and Levin (1983) found that both types of situations have occurred. They examined grants of different forms by state governments to local school districts, as well as grants provided by the federal government to state and local governments and educational agencies. They found that grants have had a significant effect on the spending patterns of grantee agencies and that this effect has varied with the type of grant involved. State aid to local school districts which was earmarked for specific purposes was found to be the most predictive of a local agency's spending pattern, because the state aid was spent on state-intended purposes.

Grantor agencies can probably never have total control over the spending patterns of grantee agencies even when grants from one level of government to another include a heavy evaluation component. After all, since local agencies continue to finance education partly from their own resources even when state control increases with a shrinking portion of local finance (Wirt 1978), state and local control are not poles of the same continuum. In other words, when state control increases by a certain amount, local control does not necessarily decrease by the same amount. Since local politics (Lutz and Iannaccone 1978) is partially independent of state politics and state finance, it has some influence on local finance. It is heavily controlled locally and may even shape state financial legislation (Zak and Glasman 1979), including that which incorporates mandated evaluation.

The data sources which form the basis for the above conjectures include, primarily, federal and state legislation and the spending patterns of local educational agencies. Very little is known about the effect of the expansion, systematization, and acceptability of evaluation on educational funding and on control of education at the local level. For that matter, very little is known about the effect of evaluation on the local educational organization. It cannot be assumed, however, that there have been no effects at the local level. Following are some preliminary conjectures.

A Multilevel Administration of Education

Until the end of the nineteenth century, the authority to control, finance, administer, and evaluate education was exercised largely by local governments. Once the reform in the authority and structure of the municipal government had begun in the twentieth century, other governments began to share in this authority (Cunningham, Hack, and Nystrand 1977; Iannaccone 1977; Campbell, Cunningham, Usdan, and Nystrand 1980). Among the new wielders of power were educational associations, state legislatures, state departments of education, the federal government, and the courts. Developments in evaluation have expanded the authority of the new power wielders and have perhaps facilitated the emergence of a new order in the administration of the educational system. This new order is reflected by the specific behaviors of the various organizations within the educational system.

The behavior of some organizations in education seems to follow the common pattern already discussed: they delegate responsibility for evaluation to others, if possible, and also provide funds if funds are available. Finally, they mandate that the funds be used for evaluation. Thus they maximize their control and ensure their survival in the midst of a high rate of change.

It seems that some organizations have been able to follow the above pattern more effectively than others. Nonlocal educational and other governmental agencies have been most successful. They have administered education largely by granting funds, although they have also certified personnel and controlled graduation requirements (Glasman 1983b). These agencies have had wide authority in financial rule making. They became highly politicized. Elected politicians have made decisions about state and federal financial aid to local school districts and about the fiscal limitations of school districts. Other government officials have implemented the political decisions in a spirit which has adhered as closely as possible to the intent of the politicians. More specifically, these agencies have legislated and allocated funds to school districts and have regulated the use of those funds. They have controlled expenditures to ensure compliance with the rules. They have also imposed financial limitations, such as minimum and maximum limits on property tax rates, property tax levies or revenue yield per student, and the growth rate of operating expenditures or the operating expenditures per student (e.g., Winkler 1979).

All this has been done in the name of the public interest, despite the resulting decline in the authority of school districts to allocate funds. This by-product seems to constitute an example of the misleading notion that nonpartisan behavior of policymakers is truly done in the public interest. How else is one to explain the increased dependence of one segment of the public — the school districts — on central government policymakers?

At the same time, the influence of local educational authorities on financial rule making has been reduced. Well-organized interest groups have influenced state and federal legislation and at times have had more power than local authorities. Since state and federal funding for education is an integral part of all publicly supported services, the number of relevant interest groups has become large indeed. Nonetheless, local educational authorities have exerted some influence, They have had the authority to make choices in their applications for nonmandated funded programs. They have also engaged in manipulating the funds they have received to conform with state and federal regulations (e.g. Shapiro 1980; Glasman 1983a).

The behavior of other organizations in education — particularly of local school districts and individual schools — has been somewhat different. These organizations have had more limited authority to delegate evaluation responsibilities to others. They have also had fewer funds to allocate and to monitor. In the use of funds, they have had more power in implementing rules than in making them. Their authority has become confined to spending state and federally allocated funds as well as locally raised funds whose limits have been imposed by the state.

The authority of local educational organizations has been significantly affected by developments in evaluation, particularly regarding personnel management. At the district level, this change has become associated with collective bargaining, appraisal, compensation, layoffs, and legal matters. At the school level, it has become associated with how rules are made and implemented. How rules are carried out has changed significantly in matters such as assigning tasks, motivating personnel to pursue those tasks, and evaluating their performance. All these activities must now be done under new conditions (Glasman 1983b).

One specific result of this increase in power at the higher level is that local educational agencies have had less control over personnel. They have had fewer formal rewards and sanctions to use, and less power to implement rules. Very little room has been left for a give-and-take relationship between district office administrators and school principals, as well as between principals and teachers. Power relationships at the local level have become problematic because they are a function of socialization in the fullest sense. They are immersed heavily in the dynamics of human relations.

In such a multicentered administration of education, several power bases exist. In theory, each center consolidates its power base and defines its limits on the basis of what it wants and what the other power bases permit. School districts and individual schools have been shaken by educational evaluation later than have nonlocal educational and other governmental agencies. But in contrast to the nonlocal agencies, local agencies have needed to adjust under powerfully imposed external conditions and without clear ways of "passing the buck" in — dollars and evaluation responsibility — to others.

Chapter *4*

The School District's Response

The first local school district was established in 1647 in Massachusetts. It had no legal form. Local school districts first acquired legal recognition in 1789 and were first empowered to raise revenues through taxes in 1801. All local public school districts today are units of local government, created by state law and empowered to administer a public school or a public educational system. About 90 percent of them are fiscally independent. They are extensions of state government and may relate directly to the federal government. They have their own governing boards, taxing power with some limitations imposed by the state, and the right to make contracts, sue, and be sued. They are not municipal corporations but rather possess quasi-corporate powers. They are either political or constitute civil divisions of the state. There were about 100,000 local school districts in the mid 1940s; today, there are less than 16,000. Their establishment, modification, consolidation, reorganization, and elimination are the result of laws enacted by state legislatures.

Local school districts may be characterized by their policies, structure, management, and decision-making patterns. Their policies reflect how they think, and their structures reflect how they are organized. Their management reflects how they function as organizations. Their decision-making patterns reflect how they influence the conduct of individual schools within their jurisdiction. The expansion and increased acceptability of systematized evaluation in education has had a profound impact on local school districts in terms of their policies, only somewhat of an impact on their structure, and a smaller

33

but still noticeable impact on their management and decision-making patterns. Overall, local school districts have adjusted, first, by preparing reports in correspondence with the evaluation mandates and, later, by also using the evaluation mandates for local purposes (Bank and Williams 1985).

Policy Changes

The intensification of societal demands for quality in education has accentuated the responsibility of educational systems to engage in systematized evaluation. That responsibility has been delegated, in the main, to local school districts. As a result, thinking at the district level has changed and now appears to be dominated by a concern for performance.

No systematic evidence exists about how districts report on externally mandated evaluation. An unsystematic examination of reporting activities in fifty school districts in eighteen states was conducted at the University of California, Santa Barbara, during the summer of 1983 (Glasman 1983d). The examination revealed only minor and insignificant differences among districts in the closeness between what a given 1982 evaluation mandate required and what the school district reported in 1983 with regard to that mandate. The reports which were examined generally followed reporting requirements closely. Neither the extensiveness of the different mandates nor the selected characteristics of the different reporting districts appear to be associated with the minor and insignificant between-district differences in reports. For example, the length and specificity of reporting requirements varied among mandates. Among the fifty districts, the average daily attendance, number of central administrators, geographical location, and percentages of revenues generated from extramural funding sources all varied. But none of these variations seem to have affected the closeness with which the actual reports followed the reporting requirements of the various mandates. In all of these districts, engagement in reporting as required by the evaluation mandates was perceived as a major added burden on school administrators. This added burden accounted for their "thinking more" about systematized evaluation.

Cuban (1984) has summarized evaluation thinking at the local school district level. His summary focuses on district policies that relate to student performance. The establishment of districtwide instructional goals, usually stated in terms of student performance, seems to be the first in a sequence of policies which a local school board adopts. Performance generally implies improvement in test scores. Next, the board revises student promotion policies to make them in accord with stated performance goals for various grade levels. In particular, graduation requirements are strengthened by making course content more substantive, by increasing the amount of class time, and by adding extra classes.

Next, the superintendent issues a mandate concerning the planning process for each of the schools in the district. The staff in each school develops schoolwide and individual classroom goals which are targeted on student performance and which are aligned with the district's goals. Simultaneously, a review of the district's curriculum is initiated. The review purports to determine the objectives for subject matter and skills. It also presumes to determine textbooks and other instructional materials, and the relevance of district tests and other tests to what is taught in the district's classrooms.

Other district policies focus more directly on staff evaluation. Revisions are undertaken in the central office for districtwide supervisory practices and evaluation instruments used with teachers and principals. The purpose is to align those instruments with goals derived from publicized research on effective teachers and principals. Districtwide evaluation programs are then revised. These programs include guidelines for collecting information on progress in reaching the goals of the district, the school, and the classroom, and for using the information to make changes.

Finally, a districtwide staff development program for teachers, principals, central office supervisors, and the school board is initiated. This program focuses on effective schools, effective teaching, effective goal development, effective assessment procedures, effective staff evaluation, and effective steps which are needed to implement each of these goals.

Structural Changes

If structure indicates how an organization as a whole functions, then local school districts have made some structural adjustments in response to the demand for more systematized evaluation. The most visible response has been the expansion of the evaluation unit in the central office of large school districts and the establishment of such a unit in smaller districts (Stufflebeam 1985).

The meaning of these units with respect to structural adjustment is not completely clear. School district structures are loosely coupled. Structural changes in the district office do not necessarily influence the internal structure of schools. Since district structures are designed to satisfy societal expectations rather than to implement specific techniques, structural changes in the district office reflect an institutional change more than a change in teaching or other techniques. Zucker (1981) argues that the control exerted by the state and the federal government has required local districts to evaluate their own activities and that the structural changes have signaled that a district has become engaged in the mandated evaluation. Zucker also argues that the signaling unit — the staff evaluation unit — can only loosely be coupled with internal organizational performance and that therefore the meaning of this unit for local purposes is uncertain.

In a survey of 265 staff evaluation units, Grunsky (1981) found that in most units the available resources were inadequate, the requirements which were imposed on the units were excessive, and the personnel training was minimal. Grunsky suggests that these attributes partially explain the high incidence of role conflict and ambiguity which surrounds the tasks of staff evaluation directors. Similar problems have been found to exist in one-person evaluation units in small districts. It may be that the structural accommodations in the form of separate staff evaluation units in central offices of school districts have placed these units in a weak position. It may be that their role is unclear. It may be that their products are questionable with respect to their utility to districtwide administrators and to school principals. Nevertheless, these separate units now exist in many school districts which did not have them in the past. Such units may adopt multiple roles, including communication, and may even influence instruction. But they are in place, and their existence has been highlighted by the school district leadership.

Changes in Management and Decision-making Patterns

The impact of systematized evaluations has been less profound on districtwide management and decision-making patterns than on districtwide policies and structure. Management represents district-wide functioning. Decision-making patterns are detected in district-wide influences on individual schools. Functioning and influences have been altered only somewhat, but even these changes are noticeable.

With regard to the management of evaluation in local school districts, the responsibility for evaluation is no longer solely in the hands of professional evaluators. District administrators have joined forces with professional evaluators to execute districtwide evaluations. This is particularly true in large school districts (Stufflebeam 1985). School district administrators and evaluators are jointly conceptualizing evaluation questions, needed information, appropriate criteria for examining the information, ways of obtaining it, report formats for communicating the findings, appropriate ways of using the findings and even such questions as how evaluation fits into the whole school district management system, including governance, operations and support, planning, and financing.

The relationship of the separate staff evaluation unit to districtwide management can be inferred only indirectly because it has not been studied systematically. Stufflebeam investigated sixteen large districts and found that in some of them the evaluation unit serves the needs of only central office administrators, while in others, it purports to serve other district administrators because it is decentralized. Stufflebeam also found that some of these sixteen districts have increased their financial allocation to fund the activities of these units during the 1970s and 1980s. Other districts have not. Currently, these allocations vary from 0.2 percent to 1.1 percent of the district's total budget. In some of the districts, the evaluation unit reports to an assistant superintendent in charge of planning, management, and evaluation. In others, it reports to a division head in charge of evaluation, testing, and data processing, who reports to an assistant superintendent in charge of instruction. In still others, it reports to a division head in charge of research, planning, and evaluation, who reports to an assistant superintendent in charge of instruction. In smaller districts, the unit reports directly to the superintendent. In none of the above cases is there a clear indication, however, whether the evaluation unit is a line or a staff unit. If these units have no line authority, then they must serve as consultants to line management. Smaller districts have smaller evaluation units, but the relationship of these units to line management in the school district is probably similar to that in larger districts (Bank, Williams, and Burry, 1981).

Even less is known about the relationship of systematized evaluation activities to districtwide decision-making patterns. What is known is that a growing number of large and medium-sized districts are moving away from specific evaluation and testing programs to systems that are analogous to management information systems (Bank and Williams 1985). Even smaller districts are establishing comprehensive data systems which can be probed by a variety of users, including not only central office administrators but also school principals and teachers. A growing number of districts of various sizes have established data-driven computerized systems which districtwide administrators think may benefit administrative and even instructional decision making.

Stufflebeam (1985) believes that these benefits are being increasingly realized. Systematized evaluation is performed to assess need. It helps maintain data bases which include school profiles and pupil censuses. It is also used to develop and assess program plans, implementation, and outcomes. In large districts, evaluation is incorporated into test development, administration, data analysis and processing, technical writing, and special evaluation studies. In some cases, it is also used in audits, curriculum assessment, and experimentation. In others, it even provides a liaison with schools, programs, and area officers.

Unpublished case studies conducted in 1984 at the University of California, Santa Barbara (Glasman 1984c), revealed that systematized evaluation performs similar functions in schools where an evaluation staff member is attached to the high school principal's office. These individuals were found to maintain data bases; assess program plans, implementation, and outcomes; and maintain a liaison with department heads and program directors in the high school. The actual influence of these individuals on the conduct of the high school could not be determined in these case studies.

Internal or External Institutionalization of Evaluation?

Are there signs that systematized evaluation is on its way to becoming institutionalized in the internal organizational structure of local school districts? To be institutionalized internally is to be an integral part of the organization's core technology (Perrow 1965) — to be "demarginalized" in the sociological sense. It is to be incorporated into the organization's core activities.

There is no evidence that this process has occurred. Neither decisions affecting individual students nor decisions affecting individual classrooms are made at the district level on the basis of systematized evaluation (Bickel and Cooley 1985). Student performance is not a direct result of decisions made by identifiable groups of district decision-makers. Rather, numerous students, teachers, and parents in numerous instances take small steps without considering the long-term consequences for the district. Learning occurs over time through a sequence of numerous, varied, small, and uncoordinated actions. These actions may eventually crystallize into a change in the overall district, but they may not. Weiss (1981) labels this process in other organizations as "decision accretion."

Neither is there much evidence that other evaluation information is systematically and explicitly employed in making decisions or in solving problems at the district level. Professional evaluators refer to systematic and explicit use of evaluation information as "instrumental use" (e.g., Weiss 1980; Leviton and Hughes 1981; Rich 1981). They do find some evidence that district decisionmakers use evaluation information to influence their thinking about an issue. Such "conceptual use" of the information may or may not lead to explicit decisions (Bickel and Cooley 1985).

An internally institutionalized function in an organization needs no promotion, no marketing, no calls for its use. Rather, it is continuously sought and exercised without much attention to its justification. Such is not the case, however, with regard to the systematized evaluation function in local school districts. In recent years, the use of systematized evaluation has been promoted vigorously, intensively, and frequently by evaluation professionals, evaluation scholars, and evaluation administrators alike.

The calls for evaluation in the late 1970s were accompanied by arguments that were based on at least two kinds of generalities. One was that districts needed evaluation (e.g., Lyon, Dorscher, McGranaham, and Williams 1978; Webster and Stufflebeam 1978; King and Thompson 1981). The other was that districts needed to align themselves with newly emerging conditions which affect them (e.g., Alkin, Daillak, and White 1979).

The calls of the 1980s have been accompanied by arguments for needs associated with governance, finances, location in the organizational hierarchy, authorities, responsibilities, and integration with decision making. In the case of governance, for example (Stufflebeam 1985), calls were made for disseminating evaluation expertise, communicating evaluation strategies, involving relevant audiences in the planning of evaluation, and communicating evaluation findings. In the case of integration with decision making, even more specific calls were made (Bickel and Cooley 1985). The typical evaluation procedure was eliminated because its conclusion-oriented and summative nature carried a negative connotation. "Decision-oriented educational research" came to take its place. Calls were made for continuous data collection and analysis activities — for "monitoring and tailoring," continuous dialogues with clients, and detailed documentation of program implementation and its redissemination.

The institutionalization of systematized evaluation outside the school district is another matter, a point which may be partially inferred from this volume's previous two chapters. The institutionalization of systematized evaluation at higher levels has been rooted in the politics of education. Evaluation of school quality and effectiveness has been added to the list of political values which currently dominate American society. It has shaken the organization of education. Intergovernmental relations have changed as the federal and state levels have responded to societal demands for educational accountability based on the quality criterion and as the local level has responded to the same federal and state demands.

It should be emphasized that the formal structures which local school districts have established or expanded to deal with the new demands have been responses more to institutional than to technological contingencies (matters of teaching techniques, etc.). These structures have become concerned more with a representation of how the district functions than with the functions themselves (Zucker 1981, p. 78). It is also possible, but still needs to be proved, that school districts have used internal evaluation to signal compliance with newly mandated rules. If true, evidence for this conjecture may be sought in the policies, structure, management, and decision making associated with districtwide evaluation activities.

If systematic evaluation is a force to be reckoned with at the school district level, it is also a phenomenon which some evaluation scholars suggest ought to be monitored with caution. They argue that its complete formalization may be impossible or, in any event, undesirable at the district level. O'Reilly (1981) suggests that only limited amounts of systematized evaluation information could ever be used in decision making and that such information would always be judged differently by different decisionmakers. The extent of its use would be minimized so long as several phenomena persist: the power of the evaluation unit remains smaller than that of the unit being evaluated; evaluation information is available from other sources; evaluation criteria are not agreed upon by all; measurement of performance is not sanctioned; and evaluation recommendations do not support outcomes that are favored by decisionmakers. The elimination of the above conditions is not at all guaranteed. Burry, Alkin, and Ruscus (1985) have suggested that systematized evaluation cannot produce quick, observable, and rational decisions and actions, and that therefore its complete formalization is hard to defend. Bank and Williams (1985) have suggested that data-driven, computerized systems which possess the potential of facilitating formalization of systematized evaluation may not be altogether compatible with an informal understanding of the evaluation function.

In summary, there is no doubt that in the 1980s evaluation has become a force which local school districts must reckon with. Pertinent data which have been collected in this regard imply that, from the perspective of local school district leaders, evaluation has so far been institutionalized much more externally than internally. How evaluation functions inside a district still depends largely on individual school leaders.

Chapter 5

Evaluation and Principals: A New Relationship

Common Roots

Evaluation may be viewed today as only one of several ways to ensure that educational objectives are achieved. Duke (1982) suggests that supervision, rewards, and sanctions are other possible forms of control. From what can be ascertained from historical accounts of education in early America, however, evaluation in education was most broadly defined to include most forms of control within organizations. In early America, school leadership and educational evaluation were one and the same. Local educators and lay persons who cared for schools shared the duties of governing and administering the schools. They led and evaluated, as well as did everything else that was needed to educate youngsters. They did so within a system of shared values which nurtured a harmony among the various tasks of running the schools. Such was the case until the end of the nineteenth century.

In the early one-teacher, one-room schools, leadership and evaluation were inseparable. Lay persons executed both functions. They worked together with the teachers to establish the curriculum, and they supervised teaching (e.g., Reeder 1951). In the early two-teacher schools, lay persons also executed both the leadership and evaluation functions, although one of the teachers was named "principal-teacher." This nomination reflected a compatability between his or her values and those of the lay nominators. The principal-teacher's nonteaching duties included taking the records to the town council.

In the later multiteacher schools, lay persons still led and evaluated but had help from two masters. The primary master, who served as school principal, was a well-recognized reading, grammar, and geography teacher. The other master, the head assistant to the school principal, was a well-recognized writing teacher. Lay leaders viewed these specialties as together constituting the central components of the curriculum — and the two masters as ensuring that these specialties were sufficiently emphasized. The masters' administrative tasks were relatively simple: they carried out lay policies inside the school.

The system of shared values continued to characterize the way schools were led and evaluated despite some significant changes in the schools themselves. The eight-grade terminal school emerged and made education a larger and more complex enterprise. When a principal was appointed to head all departments in the school, educational administration became a more specialized profession. But even as head of all departments in a larger school, the principal followed lay guidance as an administrator who coordinated the teaching function and as an evaluator who assessed the suitability of text books and the progress of students.

Even the most recent definitions of educational evaluation have their roots in the interchangeable definitions of leadership and evaluation in the nineteenth century. The purpose of administration and evaluation in the early periods was to engage in what was "considered good" and to avoid what was "considered bad." Tasks were seen as rooted in "a value stance couched in the acceptable" (Hamilton and Mort 1941; Mort 1946; Mort, Rensger, and Polley 1960). "Goodness" then was essentially identical to today's "judgment of worth or merit" (Nevo 1983). "Acceptability" then was essentially identical to today's "acceptability standards of evaluation" (Joint Committee 1981). And "shared values" then were essentially identical to today's "value orientation of evaluation" (Cronbach, et al, 1980; House 1980).

Evaluation in Education Today

Throughout the twentieth century, awareness has increased about value differences in society as a whole, as well as in the multitude of communities within the society. The same change has occurred in education. Awareness of what is good has become increasingly a function of who judges goodness, and awareness of what is acceptable has become increasingly a function of who accepts and at what social and economic price. Awareness of shared values has become, at most, an ideal which cannot be attained, and, at least, an empty rhetoric. Within these contexts, educational evaluation has changed dramatically and in a different way from school leadership. It has become a special focus of study, a value in educational politics, a destabilizing force in federal and state educational organizations, and a force to reckon with in local school districts.

Evaluation is still a new, rather than an established, specialty in education. In large educational organizations, it has established itself as a semi-institutionalized staff structural unit. In smaller educational organizations, it has attained the status of a noninstitutionalized staff unit. In either case, the new specialty is not fully integrated into management and decision-making patterns in local school districts. As a specialty, it is subservient to educational leadership in both large and small educational organizations. It is also absent as a specialty in the structural profile of individual schools.

Educational evaluation is highly publicized today, as are evaluation consultants and evaluation staff officers. Evaluation scholars and researchers find commercial publication outlets relatively easily. Evaluation interest groups are busy, and their activities are highly publicized. Evaluators and evaluation scholars are actively seeking to become part of the hard core of educational organizations. They frequently and readily advertise their accomplishments. They seek legitimation as specialists from government and educators. They ask for expanded and core funding (funding which does not have to be justified each year). They seek to increase their constituency. They train others to join their ranks. They create and try to maintain professional standards. They seek to institutionalize their specialty, but so far with limited success.

Thus the new version of evaluation has attempted to idealize the potential performance of school leaders just as had earlier notions. Rational decision making, rational problem finding and solving, and rational orientations toward task and personnel management were some of those earlier notions. Just like those, the notion of systematized evaluation has attempted to idealize leaders' potential performance because it has been in the public interest to do so. It can even be proposed that evaluation specialists want leaders to use the results of their (specialists') evaluations and to at least publicly embrace the new relationship. As it turned out, school leaders partially accepted the public appearance of a strong relationship — not necessarily with evaluation specialists directly, but with the idea that leaders should engage in outcome-based evaluation.

The Inevitability of a New Relationship

Today school principals are school leaders. They are situated in the highest formal position in the school hierarchy. The literature on educational leadership, however, does not typically deal with school leadership in any depth. It focuses, rather, on school superintendents, government officials, and educational thinkers, and even on politicians and judges (e.g., Granger 1971; Cunningham and Gephart 1973; Bridges 1977; Smith, Mazzarella, and Piele 1981; Tyack and Hansot 1982). Neither does the literature on school principals typically deal with the leadership aspect of the role in any depth (e.g., Hencley, McCleary, and McGrath 1970; Wolcott 1973; Lipham and Hoeh 1974; Olivero 1980; Roe and Drake 1980). Instead, it deals with managerial, pedagogic, political, and psychological aspects of the role without attempting to integrate these aspects into a general picture of the school principal.

Since the concept of school leadership remains vague, it is susceptible to influences from outside as well as from inside the school. In the twentieth century, educational evaluation has been one of those outside influences. It has intensified the demands on school principals for educational accountability and has helped place the school principal in the context of a multilevel administration of education. The school principal has also had to deal with evaluation as defined at the school district level.

As evaluation developed as a specialty in education, its influence on school leadership became increasingly direct. Early in the century, evaluation measured intelligence and the achievement of curriculum objectives. Its influence on school leadership was highly indirect, although school administrators' increasing concern with efficiency (Callahan 1962) was not unrelated to the measurement movement in education. Later in the century, evaluation and education moved toward a decision and policy orientation. The influence of evaluation on school leadership was still indirect but more noticeable than in the earlier years. Although not exactly known for their desire to seek and use educational research data, educational policymakers at the federal and state levels were highly influenced by evaluation directly, and they allocated new funds to local school districts and county offices of schools on the condition that evaluation requirements would be met.

Most recently, evaluation finally reached partial institutionalization at the school district level. The influence of this development on school leadership was more direct than ever before. It is not that school principals had not previously engaged in evaluation; they had. It is rather that the expansion and acceptability of systematized evaluation as a specialty in education has added to the role of school principals a new dimension. How much principals continue to do what they did before with regard to evaluation is unclear. What seems to be added, however, is a dimension of leadership which is antithetical to systematized evaluation.

This antithesis can be seen in three ways. First, although evaluation has become a political value, the role of the school principal has become apolitical. The principal is no longer free to exercise only personal judgments concerning evaluations, even though he or she can do so in other areas (e.g., Wiles, Wiles, and Bondi 1981). Second, while systematized evaluation has become a destabilizing force, the role of the principal with regard to evaluation is now perceived by federal and state officials, as well as by others outside the school, as more of a stabilizing force. Principals are viewed today as highly responsible for facilitating learning and preserving the organization. Finally, as systematized evaluation has become a force to reckon with, the role of the school principal with regard to such evaluation has not. Principals may be complying with evaluation directives, but they may also be attempting and succeeding in getting around those directives. How the directives are implemented is up to them. Principals may prefer to guard good relations with their teachers rather than risk those relations by following evaluation directives which threaten teachers.

Although it is not very clearly defined, school leadership is an established role in education. It probably cannot become a professional evaluator role because it involves a multiplicity of decisions, problem solving, and other activities which leave little time for professional evaluation. Evaluation specialists would perhaps support this contention. They would not see school principals as joining the ranks of professional evaluators because of the executive nature of the principal's role and because of their inadequate training in professional evaluation (e.g., Scriven 1967; Stufflebeam et al. 1971).

Professional evaluators would rather see school leaders as using the results of evaluation conducted by professional evaluators (e.g., Kosekoff and Fink 1982; Patton 1982; Smith 1982). But school principals have been found to be reluctant or at least hesitant to play this "user" role, particularly with regard to results of mandated and professionally conducted evaluations (Glasman 1983a). For example, such opportunities emerged when federal and state governments mandated programs that included a heavily funded external evaluation. Principals of Title I and Title VII programs were found to use the evaluation results "only incrementally" (Alkin, Daillak, and White 1979). Other principals were found to not have much interest in the specifics and to interact with evaluators informally and only about student test results (Daillak 1980). Still other principals were found to be only "somewhat" interested in results about the curriculum and "not at all" interested in results about other aspects of their schools (Stecher, Alkin, and Flesher 1981).

Principals' hesitancy about using results of evaluation conducted by outside evaluation professionals may be associated with the results themselves, particularly if those results are not what principals hoped for or wanted. But there must be other reasons for this hesitation. One may be the very mandate to have a program, as well as the very mandate to have the program evaluated, and by outsiders. In a 1984 study, principals were found to use evaluation results quite extensively when the evaluation was of programs which they thought were "most important" in their respective schools and when they took a central part in the evaluation (Glasman 1984a). In a 1982 study, principals were also found to use evaluation results quite extensively when the evaluation was of teachers and when teachers had high levels of trust and confidence in principals as evaluators (Glasman and Paulin 1982). In the 1984 study, principals were able to list very specific evaluation activities, as well as corresponding decisions. Their lists were independently confirmed by teachers in their respective schools. In the 1982 study, teachers viewed principals' day-to-day behavior as accounting for the high level of trust which they had in their principals as evaluators. It seems, then, that principals may use results of evaluation which they voluntarily conduct more readily and extensively than results of evaluation which they are ordered to conduct.

But the mandates to evaluate are there nonetheless — perhaps to stay, at least, for a while. The mandates demand that principals engage in data collection much more than they authorize principals to judge the worth of the data and to decide accordingly. School districts also require that teachers engage in data collection to a far greater extent than they provide principals with formal powers to encourage teachers to collect the data. As a result, principals are more and more uncertain how to behave (Glasman 1979a, 1979b). They appreciate the need and the value of mandated evaluation less than their district superiors do (Glasman and Bilazewski 1979; Bank, Williams, and Burry 1981).

School principals today are faced with a central dilemma with regard to mandated evaluations. On the one hand, they are pressed to incorporate "scientific" measurement as a basis for their judgments as exercised in the conduct of the schools. On the other hand, they feel that such measurement would not, in and of itself, resolve value issues raised by the quest for the use of "science" in the first place. Perhaps principals strongly believe that their own judgment is more useful for daily and hourly decision making. But they cannot publicize this judgment for fear of promoting and intensifying political debates over value issues. This no-win situation creates uncertainties and caution. As a principal, then, one may choose to continue to conduct one's own evaluation in private and comply as minimally as one can with evaluation mandates whose value one perceives as questionable!

At the same time, principals have not lost all their discretionary powers with regard to evaluation. The vagueness of their leadership role may in fact make their discretionary powers much larger than if their leadership roles were very clearly and specifically defined by state and local mandates. They own the evaluation which they conduct voluntarily, and they serve as brokers with regard to mandated evaluation. They may or may not be willing or able to separate the two evaluations and to convince teachers about their view of evaluation. But they can certainly conceptualize what they both want and can do and what they do not want to do and cannot do. At the very least, they must understand how systematization of education has influenced their leadership role and must learn what they can about the specific tasks they will face in the 1980s and may even in the 1990s.

Part II

The School Principal's Response

Today outcome-based evaluation in education is a central concern. It implies evaluation of student achievement. Its roots are in societal demands that public education be accountable for quality or effectiveness. School principals are now charged with the responsibility of gathering and reporting on student achievement data. What principals do with the data, however, is largely unknown. What they think about their use of the data for their own purposes is even less known.

Part II of this volume deals with principals' response to demands for outcome-based evaluation. The following seven chapters assume that leadership in schools today is, among other things, a function of what principals think about and do with data on student achievement. This assumption holds both promise and peril. The promise is that information about principals' use of data on student achievement will reflect what actually goes on in school leadership today. The peril is that one might mistake responses to short-term external demands for permanent changes. The following discussions are based on the hope that the promise is greater than the peril and that the difference between the two is no greater than that between what school leadership is and what it ought to be.

Chapter 6

Linking the School Principal to Student Achievement: A Review of the Literature

Ambiguities

No respectable empirical work is known which examines direct correlations between highly reliable and valid measures of school principals' attributes and valid measures of student achievement (Glasman 1984c). Had there been such a work, it would probably have employed one of two preliminary strategies.

One strategy would have hypothesized correlations between the principals' attributes and school characteristics, including levels of student achievement. The hypothesized correlates would have been regressed on one or more measures of school principals' attributes, and the direct relationship between those attributes and levels of student achievement would have been computed. As it turns out, typical empirical studies of principals do not include data on levels of student achievement (e.g., Bossart et al. 1982; Leithwood and Montgomery 1982).

The other strategy would have hypothesized, instead, correlations between school characteristics and student achievement levels. The attributes of school principals would have been included among those school characteristics. Such input-output analyses of schools have been conducted. In these analyses, the power of the inputs was estimated by variations in the outputs. Output indicators were chosen, and school characteristics and other phenomena were regressed on one or more of the output measures. Summaries of such studies reveal selected input-output associations (e.g., Levin 1970; Michelsen 1970; Katzman 1971; Cohen and Millman 1975; Murnane 1975; Bridge, Judd, and Moock 1979; Centra and Potter 1980; Glasman and Biniaminov 1981; Madaus, Airasian, and Kellaghan 1981; Walberg 1982). As it turns out, none of these summaries mentions attributes of school principals as one set of hypothesized input variables.

The absence of empirical work on the direct association between attributes of school principals and levels of student achievement is not due to lack of interest. Rather, empirical researchers probably do not believe that the association is, or even should be, a direct one. A multitude of so-called intervening variables have been conceptualized. Associations between any two or more such variables have been examined extensively.

Neither is there theoretical work on the direct influence of school principals on student achievement. This absence is also not due to lack of interest. At least three reasons may explain it. One deals with the role of principals, another with student achievement, and the third with the relationship between them.

A variety of attitudes exists about the role of school principals as school leaders, as well as about what principals do in that role (Glasman 1984c). There is simply no agreement on the one central aspect of this position. To be sure, it is often suggested that the principal's major responsibility is to improve student performance. But no theorist has suggested how the principal actually carries out this responsibility. Existing theories may be categorized into two schools of thought (Glasman 1984c). One school believes that principals are primarily educators. The school is an educational institution, and its mission is to educate students. The principal is an instructional leader, a political operator, a middleman, and an innovator. The other theory is that principals are primarily administrators. As such, they exercise authority, plan, implement, coordinate, and evaluate.

The absence of theoretical work on the direct influence of principals on student achievement may have another reason, this one involving student achievement. A variety of attitudes exists on what constitutes student achievement, what indicators of it should be measured, and how. A few people believe that achievement is ability and should be measured in relation to a norm. A larger minority of thinkers also believes that achievement is ability, but thinks it should be measured against certain criteria. A majority believes that achievement is the acquisition of skills and knowledge in specific subject areas and that it should be measured by tests which pertain to those specific areas. According to this belief, a profile of achievement must take into account specific curricula, abilities of individual students, and test standardization.

The third possible reason for the absence of theoretical work on the direct influence of principals on student achievement deals with the relationship itself. Most of the work on determinants of student achievement has focused not on principals but on learners and learning paths, including ability and motivation, cognition, and emotions, to mention only a few broadly conceived areas. Other work has focused on the classrooms — their composition, dynamics, learning time, and use of educational materials. Some work has also focused on educational and school programs. And in more recent years, there has been work on organizational aspects of the school, including their authority structures, climates, communication, and interpersonal relations.

When these three reasons are considered together, the absence of a clear relationship between attributes of school principals and levels of student achievement becomes thoroughly understandable. A multitude of indicators exists for both principals' attributes and student achievement. And a multitude of intervening variables exists between them. But there are disagreements about the concepts, their indicators, and their measures.

There are additional problems as well. Theorists hypothesize numerous exogenous causes of principals' attributes, of student achievement, and of their intervening variables. One such factor is a student's background which is unrelated to the school. Another is the policies which are generated for the school but from an external source. No wonder, then, that the link between school principals and levels of student achievement is highly complex and indirect.

Research on High-Performance Schools

In recent years, student test scores have declined, and a growing number of people have come to believe that schools should do something to reverse this trend. These developments have given rise to the so-called effective school research. Researchers have assumed that they can detect, delineate, and measure phenomena in schools which correlate with high student achievement. Armed with this assumption, they have identified schools whose students' aggregate achievement level is higher than that of the national, state, or local averages. They have used norm-referenced and other scores of student achievement to identify those schools. The general research objective has been to identify the characteristics common to those schools.

Several such characteristics have been found, among them a relatively long study time, a strong emphasis on basic skills, considerable attention to student order and discipline, a high expectation by teachers with regard to student achievement, and a strong emphasis on systematic evaluation of student progress. These characteristics have also included the so-called effective school leadership attributes: the establishment of positive school climates, the initiation of goal-focused activities, and the emphasis on the efficacy and efficiency of school improvement.

However, the centrality of "effective school leadership" in determining "high student achievement" has been viewed by "effective school researchers" with caution. They have recognized, for example, that teachers have more to do with school improvement than have principals (Mackenzie 1983). They have also recognized that improvement should be examined not only in association with high achievers but also in association with low achievers (Frederiksen and Edmonds 1979). Finally, they have acknowledged that improvement is perceived differently by different personnel in schools (McCarthy, Lazarus, and Canner 1980).

Nonetheless, "effective school researchers" have viewed school leadership as an independent variable which does improve levels of student achievement as measured by achievement scores (e.g., Weber 1971; State of New York 1974; Madden et al. 1978; Brookover et al. 1979; Rutherford and Hoffman 1981). Thus, principals who are considered "effective leaders" are found to emphasize student achievement, set corresponding instructional strategies, provide orderly atmospheres, evaluate student progress frequently, coordinate instructional programs which focus on enhancing student achievement, and support teachers strongly and consistently. These principals are said to have a "strong student achievement orientation," which they implement through a "tight" management process (e.g., Cohen 1981; Hall et al. 1984). The major contribution of the "effective school research" with regard to effective school leadership is, perhaps, that it has highlighted this last-mentioned fundamental characteristic. A strong student achievement orientation implies a strong belief that enhancement of student achievement is a central goal of the school. A corresponding tight management process implies the initiation and maintenance of a framework within which that strong belief can be implemented.

In other respects, however, the contribution of the "effective school research" on the link between principals' attributes and student achievement levels remains largely unclear. Was this fundamental characteristic discovered, for example, as a result of the "effective school research," or was it assumed at the start that the intent of the research was to provide empirical support for the assumption? In connection with this question, others can also be asked: Why were only schools with high achievers selected for examination in most studies? Can "effective school leadership behavior" be emulated by principals who lead "ineffective schools"? Additional findings complicate matters further. Principals in "ineffective schools," for example, do not differ significantly from principals in "effective schools" and in some cases even exhibit stronger "leadership patterns" than principals in " effective schools" (e.g., State of New York 1974; Ellis 1975; Wellisch et al. 1978; Phi Delta Kappa 1980). Such findings have raised doubts about viewing principals in terms of student achievemen in any way, and especially about evaluating principals on the basis of student achievement. Some writers have argued that school leadership must be conceptualized in broader terms, including the ability to satisfy individuals in the school, and competency in various situations (e.g., Duke and Imber 1983).

The Question of How Principals Use Student Achievement Data

Although the connection between principals' leadership attributes and levels of student achievement is indirect and complex, the fundamental characteristic of effective leadership just highlighted may clarify the link somewhat. A tight management process that is oriented toward student achievement must use data on student achievement. After all, these data are a resource. Exactly what data principals use, how they use it, and for what purposes may help describe and possibly also explain not only principals' student achievement orientation but also what they actually do to improve student achievement.

The choice of such a focus is predicated on several assumptions. One is that these data are available for principals to use. In several states, they are indeed available. In some states, such as in California, principals are even required to collect these data and to report them to their district offices and elsewhere. A second assumption is that principals have some authority to use student achievement data. A third assumption is that principals exercise some measure of control over how the data are used.

The control which principals have over the use of student achievement data depends upon their formal as well as informal authority to use the data. Their formal authority is spelled out relatively clearly by law and by state and local bylaws. Their informal authority is not. If principals do not confuse the data with what the data represent, they may have a great deal of informal control over it. If they do confuse the two, their level of control may be low. For example, if student achievement does not improve, principals may think they have failed. The fear of failure may make them fearful of using achievement data altogether.

A way to reduce this fear is to view the data as a resource and the work with the data as experimental (e.g., Argyris 1983). Principals may then have more informal control over what they do with the data, at least more than over actual student performance. After all, they have much more control over what is done with achievement data than over what gets done with students.

How principals exercise control over what gets done with student achievement data also deserves some elaboration. This control is highly dependent upon their perceptions. Every perception has a consequence, regardless of whether it is true or false (e.g., Langer 1983). To think that one has little control is to have a relatively low sense of one's effectiveness. Conversely, to perceive that one has a relatively high level of control is to possess a sense of a relatively high degree of confidence in one's effectiveness.

Principals' confidence in their control over what gets done with data on student achievement can be increased in several ways. They may first adopt improvement in student achievement as an important value (Weick 1982). They may then communicate this attitude to teachers and students (Sproull 1979; Natriello and Dornbusch 1980–1981). Then they may personally exchange resources with teachers and students about this value (Ouchi 1980). Specifically, they may adopt the value stance that these data will help enhance student achievement. They can then judge the worth of the data for a variety of decisions which they may make and for a variety of corresponding actions which they may take.

These steps alone, however, do not solve the problem. Although principals may exercise a relatively high degree of control over what gets done with data on student achievement, what in fact gets done with the data may be relatively far removed from the most immediate determinants of student achievement. And although they may exercise a relatively low degree of control over what gets done with the data, what in fact gets done may be relatively close to the most immediate determinants of student achievement.

Every principal, for example, can proclaim that he or she strongly believes that the central goal of the school is to improve achievement. Nowhere does it say that principals cannot inform teachers about this central goal — in fact, they are encouraged to do so. But such words alone may or may not be associated with actual student achievement; they are certainly very far removed from what actually determines student performance.

An example of the opposite situation is when principals actually take on specific responsibilities for designing and implementating instructional techniques on the basis of student achievement data and force teachers to employ those techniques. Principals participate in such activities, if at all, with extreme caution. Their discretionary powers in this regard are limited by the highly autonomus status accorded to teachers in what they do behind the classroom doors. But for principals to become involved in such activities is to move closer to actual control over student achievement.

This irony is a source of frustration for principals. The level of frustration, in and of itself, may influence their perception of control, as well as their overall sense of effectiveness. But it stands to reason that principals understand this ironic interplay and that their actual use of data on student achievement for purposes of improving student achievement is full of compromises.

The next six chapters present an outline of a study which focused on principals' attitude toward student achievement and their use of student achievement data.

Chapter 7

Introduction to a Statewide Study of Elementary School Principals

Exploratory Field Data

Principals must have a realistic orientation toward student achievement if they are to be effective leaders. The "effective schools research" identified two broad elements of this orientation: a belief that enhancing student achievement is a central goal of schools, and the creation and maintenance of a framework for implementing this belief. Within this broad orientation, the principal must make specific choices. Those choices must also be realistic if they are to be useful.

Exploratory investigations have identified some elements associated with principals' orientation toward data on student achievement. One investigation was conducted in the early 1980s at the Center for the Study of Evaluation in the University of California, Los Angeles. The center collected data on principals' and teachers' perceptions about principals' engagement in administering achievement tests to students and about their follow-up activities. It found that, nationwide, secondary school principals were devoting more time than elementary school principals to these tasks (Dorr-Bremme 1983).

A concurrent investigation, conducted in the University of California, Santa Barbara, sought data on school principals only in California. Here too, elementary school principals were found to devote less time than secondary school principals to the administration of achievement tests. The investigation conducted in Santa Barbara also found that much more pressure is exerted on elementary than on secondary school principals to increase their personal involvement in this task. All elementary school principals surveyed were reporting the data generated from these tests to their respective district offices, but only 15 percent were using the data "extensively" and "formally" for internal school purposes. The findings in this investigaion were generated by telephoning the 33 largest unified school districts in California, 28 responses were received (Glasman 1981).

In the spring of 1982, a third exploratory investigation was conducted by the University of California, Santa Barbara. Fifty-one elementary school principals in California were telephoned. All were acquaintences of the author. These principals were asked about how extensively they used student achievement data. All 51 principals said that they report the data to their respective district offices. All said that they make "at least some other use of the data," but only 13 reported "some other formal use of the data." and only 7 reported "extensive formal use of the data." All but 2 of the 51 said that they were "uncertain about their formal authority to use the data as they see fit."

These principals identified four possible ways in which they might use student achievement data. The first was to fulfill schoolwide instructional objectives. Two-thirds of the principals said that they had been required by their districts to try to integrate student achievement data into the design of those objectives. The second was to evaluate programs. Over one-half of the principals said that student achievement data were central to program evaluation. The third was their general interaction with teachers and, more specifically, their evaluation of teachers. All but one of the principals said that the usefulness of student achievement data in evaluating teachers is "varied" but also "ambiguous." The fourth was solving student achievement problems. All the principals said that student achievement data are most important and that they spend quite a bit of their time trying to solve achievement problems.

Exploratory Review of the Literature

As a result of these exploratory field studies, a review of the literature was launched at the University of California, Santa Barbara, to detect more specific concepts which might characterize principals' attitudes toward student achievement, as well as toward their use of student achievement data. The results are grouped by the four topics just discussed.

First, the literature emphasizes the importance of fulfilling instructional objectives, as well as the central role of principals in the development of those objectives, particularly in basic skills. Hertzberg (1984) summarizes the literature in the form of a loop. If principals establish clear and specific achievement-related instructional objectives, then they should be able to influence teachers to try to reach those objectives. If teachers do so, then they should be able to help monitor student progress toward those objectives. Monitoring, in turn, should facilitate the development of tests that should give them feedback on student progress. If tests are administered, and if feedback is provided to teachers, then teachers should be able to use the data to maintain or modify the instructional objectives which were originally developed.

Hertzberg establishes this loop in the form of assumptions. The literature provides for nothing more than assumptions. At least three conditions may guide further research on this subject. One is the extent to which principals believe in these assumptions. Another is how they perceive their success in resolving practical issues on the basis of the assumptions. A third is the way they perceive the evaluation of the outcome of their efforts. For principals' responses to these questions, see chapter 8.

Very little is discussed in the literature about how principals use achievement data to evaluate programs. (Hoy and Miskel 1982; Kmetz and Willower 1982). But principals are now required to report to the district office on program evaluation, and the reports must include data on student achievement (O'Reilly 1981). In this regard, there are issues associated with programs that are controversial and with ways to evaluate such programs (Sax 1974; Mitchell and Spady 1978).

At least three concepts emerge which can guide research on how principals use student achievement data to evaluate programs. One is that principals believe in using the data in program evaluation. Another is that they believe in using the data in evaluation reports, and a third is that they believe in using the data in reports about controversial programs. The corresponding actual use of the data in these three instances is also of interest. For research on these concepts, see chapter 9.

Principals' leadership in their interactions with teachers is discussed extensively in the literature, as is their specific role in using student achievement data to evaluate teachers. Liebman (1984) has summarized this literature from two perspectives. In one, he focuses on the theories of teacher evaluation (e.g., Howsam 1960; Popham 1971; Alkin and Klein 1972; Lewis 1973; Coats 1975; Stow 1979; Thomas 1979; Goldhammer, Anderson and Krajewski 1980; Sergiovanni 1982). In another, he focuses on the role of principals in teacher evaluation and particularly on their use of student achievement data. The latter subject is surrounded by ambiguities (e.g., Bidwell 1965, 1977; Cohen, March, and Olsen 1972; Bidwell and Kasarda 1975; Lortie 1975; Mitchell and Spady 1978; Duckworth 1979a; Edmonds 1981; Sweeney 1982; Weick 1982; Purkey and Smith 1983).

Particularly significant are the arguments for and against the evaluation of teachers on the basis of student achievement data. The position which supports it rests on essentially three views. One is that such data constitute one of several valuable sources (Niedermeyer and Klein 1972; Herman 1973; Ebel 1979). Another is that the data constitute a measurable output of teachers' efforts (Ebel 1979; Millman 1981; Pohland and Cross 1982). The third is that a correlation exists between effective schools and high student achievement. The position which opposes evaluation of teachers on the basis of student achievement rests on essentially two views. One is that student achievement data as measured by common tests have validity problems (Coleman et al., 1966; Bridge, Judd, and Moock 1979; Baker and Quellmalz 1980; Kellaghan, Madaus, and Airaisian 1982). Another is that the relationship between teacher performance and student achievement is insufficiently strong to justify using student data to evaluate teachers (Howsam 1960; Glass 1974; Bridge, Judd, and Moock 1979; Baker and Quellmalz 1980; Millman 1981).

The literature on this subject is so extensive and contradictory that only a few concepts were chosen from it to guide the research. One concept relates to how principals share student achievement data with teachers. A second relates to how they use the data to evaluate teachers, and the third relates to the value of such use in influencing teaching. For research on these beliefs and actions, see chapter 10.

School principals probably spend a significant portion of their time attempting to solve academic problems. The literature on this subject is extensive but focuses primarily on principals' interactions with teachers. Emphasis is placed on goals and production (e.g., Brookover et al. 1979), power and decision making (e.g., Olivero 1980), and organization and control of instruction (e.g., Wellisch et al. 1978). The literature also focuses on principals' roles in determine class size and composition (e.g., Rosenholz and Wilson 1980) and on grouping of students for instructional purposes (e.g., Calfee and Brown 1979). However, it does not do so in any depth, certainly not as much as it deals with learning and teaching themselves (e.g. Stallings 1980). Clues are provided primarily by the "effective schools research."

Two key concepts which emerge from the literature are the "proactiveness" and strength of principals' involvement in dealing with the academic problems of low achievers. Proactivity is central in two stages of involvement. One is the stage of becoming aware of the problem; the other is the stage of attempting to solve it. The next question is how deeply the principal will become involved, and in what specific ways he or she will act. (For relevant research, see chapter 11.)

Sample of Principals Surveyed

On the basis of the preliminary field investigations, the researchers decided that the California study should be limited to elementary school principals. Elementary school principals were found to be under stronger pressure to become more personally involved in achievement tests. They were required to report results to their respective district offices but were not necessarily using the data extensively and formally within their schools. They reported some use, a strong belief that they should use tests more, but also uncertainties about their formal authority to use tests.

There were other reasons for limiting the survey to elementary school principals at this stage. Since these principals are the only administrators in their schools, they are closer to students and are more aware of performance than are secondary school principals . In addition, the literature emphasizes their role in student learning more than it emphasizes the role of secondary school principals.

It was also decided that principals in only elementary school districts should be surveyed. It was reasoned that elementary school principals in unified districts might not be as preoccupied with only elementary schools as their colleagues in elementary districts. In other words, they might also be concerned with realities in junior and senior high schools in their districts.

The population of principals had to be limited because of the limited resources available for the study. Therefore the study tried to select a range of perceptions about principals' effectiveness. Several criteria were considered as the endpoints of the range. The final choice was how closely the principals adhered to the district's philosophy about student achievement enhancement. In the survey, then, the principals' immediate supervisors were asked to identify the "most" and the "least" effective principals. No attempt was made to determine whether the principals were in fact effective or ineffective.

The study surveyed only principals in districts which included between 6 and 18 schools. It was reasoned that supervisors of principals in larger districts might not know each principal sufficiently well, and that those in smaller districts might not be able to easily differentiate and nominate principals at the two endpoints in the range.

In the summer of 1982, California had 151 K-6 school districts with 6 to 18 schools. From preliminary telephone calls to supervisors, it became apparent that the supervisors were not prepared to nominate with confidence more than two principals at either endpoint of the range. Resources were availble to survey no more than 400 principals. Therefore a random sample of only 95 districts (63 percent) was chosen. The districts in the sample and those in the entire population of 151 were comparable in terms of the number of schools they had (see table 7.1).

Superintendents of each of the sample districts were personally telephoned in the fall of 1982 by two doctoral students at the University of California, Santa Barbara, who also served as assistant district superintendents in two such districts in California. The superintendents were first asked whether they personally supervised elementary school principals. If they did, the conversation was continued. If they did not, the interviewers contacted the appropriate district administrator who did supervise elementary school principals. Once the supervisor was identified, the person was told about a survey regarding principal leadership.

Seven supervisors declined to be involved in the study after they heard that the study dealt with the "most" and "least" effective prin-

Table 7.1   Number of Schools in a California Elementary School District

Number of schools in a district	Percentage of sample	
	Entire population (151 districts)	Random sample (95 districts)
6	18	19
7	14	12
8	11	13
9	11	10
10	10	9
11	6	9
12	7	9
13	3	3
14	3	5
15	8	5
16	0	1
17	6	4
18	2	2

cipals. Four of the 7 were concerned that confidentiality might be breached, even though confidentiality was ensured. They were especially concerned about identifying the least effective principals. All 4 said that some least effective principals were either being reassigned or terminated from their present positions. Three other supervisors said that it was inappropriate to solicit this type of information by telephone without first providing an abstract of the study, including a copy of the survey questionnaire to the district superintendent. As a result, only 88 of the 95 sample districts participated in the study.

All 88 supervisors were presented with the same information. Specifically, two terms were defined. The first was *student achievement gains*, which was specified as

> . . . how students have progressed as measured by a variety of formal and informal tests and student work. Measures of these gains can include, but are not limited to, standardized norm-referenced tests and criterion-referenced tests, school and district-made tests, and student work evaluated and graded by teachers.

The second term, *principal effectiveness in enhancing student achievement gains*, was specified as

> . . . levels of impact a principal has on student achievement at his or her school.

Supervisors were asked to nominate the following:

(1) the principal who demonstrated the greatest effectiveness in enhancing student achievement gains in his or her school;

(2) the principal who demonstrated the least effectiveness;

(3) the principal who demonstrated the next greatest effectiveness; and

(4) the principal who demonstrated the next least effectiveness.

They nominated 185 individuals for (1) and (3) and 117 individuals for (2) and (4).

Surveys were mailed to all 302 principals who were identified. The survey covered the use of student achievement data in dealing with instructional objectives, in evaluating programs, in evaluating teachers, and in improving student performance. A typed letter (Dilman 1978), was attached to the survey, and the name of the principal's supervisor was included. The first mailing was on May 4, 1983. A printed postcard was mailed on May 13, 1983, to all 302 principals to thank those who had returned the survey and to ask others to please do so. A thank-you card was mailed on May 20, 1983, to all those who responded to the second mailing. At that point 62 percent of the principals had responded.

On May 27, 1983, another letter was mailed to the other 38 percent of the principals explaining the importance of the study and asking them to respond. By June 3, 1983, an additional 21 percent had responded and had been thanked by a postcard. On June 3, 1983, another letter was sent to the other 17 percent. The content of this letter was similar to the one mailed on May 27, 1983. It was sent by certified mail and included another copy of the survey. By June 17, 1983, an additional 12 percent had responded and been thanked by a postcard. At that point, 271 principals had responded. They included 174 of 185 (94 percent) of the "most effective group" and 97 of 117 of the "least effective group" (83 percent).

The questionnaire also included questions about sex, age, and years as principal. For these data, see table, 7.2.

Table 7.2   Elementary School Principals' Responses on Sex, Age, and Years in Office

Question	Response			Entire population[c]
	Group 1[a]	Group 2[b]	Total	
Sex (percent males)	67	93	76	69[d]
Age				
<40	23	7	17	18[e]
40–49	40	30	46	46[e]
Years in office				
1–4	27	7		
5–9	29	13		
10–14	12	23		
15–19	19	32		
20–24	8	12		
≥25	5	12		

[a] Principals nominated by supervisors as "most effective" (174 principals).

[b] Principals nominated by supervisors as "least effective" (97 principals).

[c] For state of California: 3,522 principals in 151 school districts.

[d] Sex comparability between sample and the entire population was high $(x^2 = 6.228; 0.01 < p < 0.025)$.

[e] Age comparability between the sample and the entire population was high $(x^2 = 0.279; p < 0.5)$.

Limitations of the Study

The elements chosen for the California study evolved from the literature and the exploratory field studies. Although this process is not uncommon with research on educational leadership or on educational evaluation, in this case it produced only general conclusions. From an experimental perspective, the results cannot be considered completely unambiguous.

One of the reasons for this ambiguity is that the California study relied exclusively on self-report data. These data constitute nothing more than written responses to questions, and as such have reliability and validity problems. In addition, the statistical analyses used in the study were appropriate for testing the probability of differences between the two groups of principals; where these analyses were used to compare items, however, the discussions were only preliminary and suggestive in nature.

Another limitation is that multiple t-tests were used to compare means without attempts to adjust the criterion level. These tests fail to account for intercorrelations among the elements tested ("type A error"). However, the elements in this study were conceived in a broad sense only. Further investigations may try to transform these elements into more specific variables and into clearer indicators of those variables. Only then should the elements be considered multiple dependent measures in comparing groups, and a multivariate analysis should then be conducted.

Internal consistency reliability estimates were reported for the grouping of questions on instructional objectives (see chapter 8). The grouping of questions on the other three topics (chapters 9, 10, and 11) was not founded on hard-tested concepts. Comparisons among groups of items in these chapters were without value and therefore were not done.

Finally, not all the statistically significant differences which were detected were large enough to be useful. Only some of the mean differences provided meaningful insights. For a summary of the study and a discussion of those insights, see chapter 12.

Chapter 8

School Leadership and Instructional Objectives

Questions

Instruction is the heart of school services and is guided by specific instructional objectives, at least in theory. Those objectives are therefore a central concern of school leaders. In dealing with instructional objectives, the principal is limited by dictates handed down from the school district administration and by teachers' discretionary powers. Within these limits, principals assume a variety of leadership tasks. They may devise plans for developing instructional objectives, help develop the plans, and encorage teachers to follow them. They may supervise instruction, monitor the outcome of teaching to instructional objectives, and facilitate the use of outcome data for further work on those objectives.

The accomplishment of these tasks rests on several assumptions, and the first purpose of the study was to examine principals' beliefs in those assumptions. The first two fundamental assumptions are that

(1) student learning can be reduced to specific instructional objectives; and

(2) principals can influence teachers to teach to specific instructional objectives.

Unless one makes these assumptions, the entire process of leadership in the area of instructional objectives is a meaningless concept. Other, somewhat less fundamental, assumptions are also relevant to the process of leadership in this area. Various segments of society are demanding improvement in basic skills. A corresponding assumption, therefore, is that

(3) teaching to specific instructional objectives in the basic skills can improve student achievement.

Society is also pointing to school principals as leaders who should be able to improve student achievement. A corresponding assumption here is that

(4) principals can have an impact on student achievement in the basic skills.

Some measures are needed to ascertain specific gains in levels of student achievement. Data on student achievement constitute one such measure. Therefore, a corresponding assumption is that

(5) specific instructional objectives in the basic skills areas can be influenced by data on student achievement in those areas.

A second purpose of the study was to examine principals' perceptions about what they have accomplished in integrating student achievement data with specific instructional objectives in the basic skills. A pilot study revealed four sets of issues which principals face. It found that pressure was exerted on principals by the district administration to formalize, specify, clarify, and measure instructional objectives. It was not at all clear, however, what principals thought they had achieved in these four areas. The study therefore asked principals how they felt they succeeded in resolving the following four issues:

(6) the extent to which the school has formalized its student achievement data-based instructional objectives;

(7) the extent to which those objectives have been specified;

(8) the extent to which those objectives have been made clear to teachers; and

(9) the extent to which student achievement has been measured as a function of the school's instructional objectives.

These four questions did not attempt to examine the actual success with which principals resolved the corresponding four sets of issues. Rather, they focused on principals' perceptions of their success.

The third central purpose of the study was to examine how principals perceived the outcome of their leadership efforts. Teachers' discretionary powers behind the closed classroom doors permit an examination of only two kinds of outcomes. One is teachers' actual instruction. The other is teachers' accountability. Thus, the study asked principals about the following:

(10) the extent to which teachers actually use the school's specific instructional objectives to guide instruction; and

(11) the extent to which teachers are individually held accountable for student achievement on the basis of those objectives.

Another subject that is associated with the outcome of the principals' leadership efforts pertains to what principals do behind the closed school yard gates. Thus, the study also asked principals about how they viewed

(12) the degree to which the principal ("you") is held accountable by the district office for student achievement on the basis of instructional objectives.

This study, then, examined three sets of principals' perceptions about their leadership in dealing with instructional objectives. The first set (questions 1–5)) focused on their beliefs in the theoretical assumptions associated with that leadership. How strongly they believed in the assumptions was viewed as one clue to what they do. The second set (questions 6–9) focused on how well they think they have succeeded in resolving central issues associated with the execution of their leadership. This success was viewed as one indicator of what they actually do. The third set focused on how they evaluate the outcome of what they do. This evaluation would indicate (a) the results of what they do (question 10); (b) what they do with the results (question 11); and (c) what the district does with the results (question 12).

Responses

Principals responded according to a 7-point rating scale to indicate the strength of their belief in an assumption or a perception. The questions were preceded by the following paragraph:

> The survey is concerned with student achievement gains in your school. We define gains made by students as measured by a variety of tests and student work. The following questions deal with student learning associated with reading, mathematics, and language basic skills programs in your school. Please circle the number on the response scale which most accurately reflects how strongly you feel about each item.

The means and standard deviations of responses of each group of principals ("most" and "least" effective) are presented in table 8.1 for each of the 12 questions. As can be seen, all the means are above the midpoint on the response scale. Some principals in each group responded below the midpoint on the scale, particularly on question 10 ("what teachers do") and question 11 ("the extent to which principals hold them individually accountable"). If a mean response above the midpoint is assumed to be a positive response, a response at the midpoint a neutral response, and a response below the midpoint a negative response, then all the means and standard deviations reflect positive beliefs about these assumptions and perceptions.

The relatively lower positive means on questions 10 and 11 for both groups of principals prompted the hypothesis that principals are less confident in what teachers do and the extent to which teachers are held accountable than they are in all other items in the questionnaire. This hypothesis was then tested. The responses to each of the 12 questions for each group of principals were standardized within each of four groups of questions: the group on assumptions, the group on success, the group made up of questions 10 and 11, and the group comprising only question 12. T-tests were applied between each of the four groups of questions separately for each group of principals. A ≤ 0.05 level of

Table 8.1 Responses of Principals to Questions Concerning Instructional Objectives

Question group	Question	Response (1 = low; 7 = high)			
		Group 1[a]		Group 2[b]	
		Mean	Standard deviation	Mean	Standard deviation
Assumptions	1. Can student learning be reduced to specific instructional objectives?	5.90	1.12	5.77	1.07
	2. Can principals influence teachers to teach to those objectives?	5.91	0.98	5.43	1.15
	3. Can teaching to those objectives in basic skills improve student achievement?	6.20	0.84	5.40	1.01
	4. Can principals have an impact on student achievement in basic skills?	5.69	0.82	5.43	0.92
	5. Can objectives in basic skills be influenced by student achievement?	5.92	1.02	5.90	1.06
Perceptions of success	6. Has the school formalized its student achievement data-based instructional objectives?	5.62	1.15	5.65	1.17
	7. Have those objectives been specified?	5.72	1.00	5.64	0.98
	8. Are those objectives clear to teachers?	5.61	1.02	5.62	0.93
	9. Is student achievement measured as a function of those objectives?	5.79	1.00	5.64	0.99
Evaluation of results	10. Do teachers actually use the school's objectives to guide instruction?	5.09	1.01	4.85	1.06
	11. Are teachers individually held accountable for student achievement on the basis of those objectives?	4.93	1.34	4.83	1.26
	12. Are principals held accountable by the district for student achievement on the basis of those objectives?	5.25	1.43	5.49	1.28

[a] Principals nominated by supervisors as "most effective" (174 principals).

[b] Principals nominated by supervisors as "least effective" (97 principals).

significance was sought. Confidence intervals were calculated to confirm the levels of significance.

Figure 8.1 displays the findings for group 1, and figure 8.2 for group 2. As can be seen from the two figures, two significant differences were common to both groups of principals. One was between the group of questions on assumptions and questions 10 and 11. The other was between the groups of questions on success and questions 10 and 11. Both groups of principals seem to have significantly less confidence in the evaluation of the outcome of their leadership in terms of teacher follow-up and teacher accountability than they do in assumptions underlying their leadership or in their success in having executed their leadership. Because these differences were significant for both groups of principals, it is highly possible that they exist in the minds of all elementary school principals in California who are employed in elementary school districts.

Analysis

The data reveal some apparent contradictions. Principals were found to have relatively little confidence in their ability to actually influence teaching and to hold teachers accountable. Yet they were relatively confident of their leadership ability and effectiveness. This inconsistency may indicate that principals become frustrated when they do not view the outcome as positively as they view their efforts.

Apparently, the two groups of principals find ways to reduce this frustration differently. The confidence of the first group in their own accountability (question 12) was as low as their confidence in their teachers' accountability (questions 10 and 11), and was also significantly lower than their confidence in their own efforts (questions 1–5, 6–11). Thus, they may be less uncomfortable with the inconsistency between a high confidence in their efforts and a low confidence in the accountability of all involved. This was not the case in the second group of principals. Their confidence in their own accountability (question 12) was as high as their confidence in their own efforts (questions 1–5, 6–11). Thus, they may be less uncomfortable with the inconsistency between a high confidence in their efforts and corresponding accountability and a low confidence in teachers' efforts.

The data which support these statements are as follows. For the first group of principals, the difference between the mean response on questions 10 and 11 combined and that on question 12 was insignificant. For the second group of principals, it was significant. In addition, for the second group of principals, the difference between the mean response on question 12 and that on questions 1 through 5 and 6 through 11 combined was insignificant, whereas for the first group of principals, it was significant.

The sample as a whole revealed the following range of perceptions:

(1) confidence in assumptions underlying leadership is higher than confidence in one's success;

(2) confidence in one's success is higher than confidence in one's accountability; and

(3) confidence in one's own accountability is higher than confidence in teacher accountability.

Confidence in the assumptions underlying leadership varied considerably. The difference between the means of the two groups of principals was significant (p ≤ 0.02) on questions 2, 3 and 4 (see table 8.2). The widest range was on question 3, which had to do with teachers' efforts; the other two questions had to do with principals' efforts. The difference between the means of the two groups of principals was significant (p $= 0.002$) on questions 1,2,3,4, and 5 combined (see table 8.3). The differences between the means of the two groups of principals on each of the other three groups of items were not significant.

The importance of the assumptions underlying leadership in the development of instructional objectives was emphasized at the beginning of this chapter. The wide range among principals in the strength of their belief in these assumptions may be the key to a deeper understanding of this aspect of leadership because these assumptions may have the most bearing on actual levels of student achievement. Of all the aspects of school leadership, the development of instructional objectives is the most closely connected to student achievement.

Figure 8.1

Differences between Mean Responses of 174 "Most Effective" Principals

to Four Groups of Questions Concerning Instructional Objectives

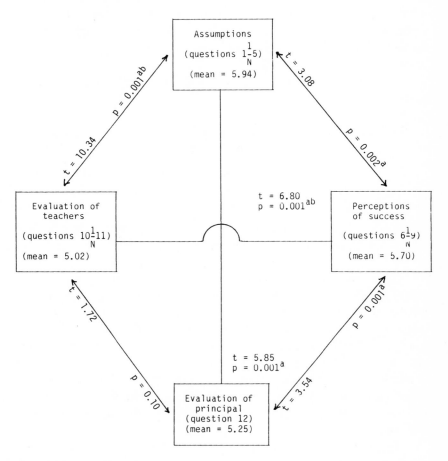

[a] Significant difference.

[b] Also significant in group 2 ("least effective" principals).

Figure 8.2

Differences between Mean Responses of 97 "Least Effective" Principals

to Four Groups of Questions Concerning Instructional Objectives

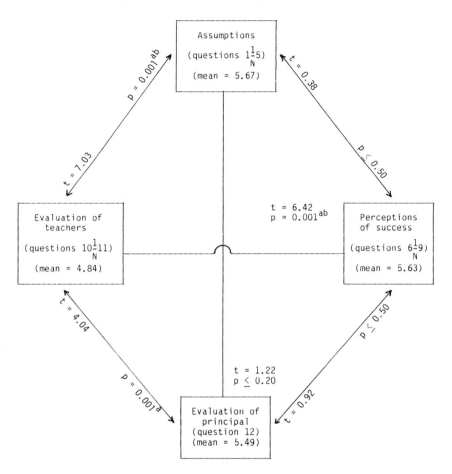

^{a} Significant difference.

^{b} Also significant in group 1 ("most effective" principals).

Table 8.2 Significant Differences between Mean Responses of Principals to Questions 2, 3, and 4

Question	Mean of Group 1[a]	Mean of Group 2[b]	t	P
2. Can principals influence teachers to teach to specific instructional objectives?	5.91	5.43	3.47	0.001
3. Can teaching to specific instructional objectives in basic skills improve student achievement?	6.20	5.40	2.45	0.02
4. Can principals have an impact on student achievement in basic skills?	5.69	5.43	2.32	0.02

Note: Scale is 1 to 7, where 1 = low and 7 = high.

[a] Principals nominated by supervisors as "most effective" (174 principals).

[b] Principals nominated by supervisors as "least effective" (97 principals).

Table 8.3 Differences between mean Responses of Principals to Four Groups of Questions

Question group	Group 1[a]			Group 2[b]				
	Alpha for interitem correlations	Mean	Standard deviation	Alpha for interitem correlations	Mean	Standard deviation	t	P
Assumptions	0.816	5.940	0.631	0.784	5.674	0.713	3.167	0.002
Perceptions of success	0.877	5.702	0.830	0.780	5.629	0.761	0.730	0.500
Evaluation of teachers	0.628	5.023	1.010	0.588	4.835	0.937	1.529	0.200
Evaluation of principal	Only one item	5.246	1.434	Only one item	5.485	1.284	1.406	0.200

Note: Scale is 1 to 7, where 1 = low and 7 = high.

[a] Principals nominated by supervisors as "most effective" (174 principals).

[b] Principals nominated by supervisors as "least effective" (97 principals).

Chapter *9*

School Leadership and Program Evaluation

Questions

Demands for accountability in education have been transformed into mandates to evaluate programs and to report on those evaluations. The mandates have emphasized that data on student achievement be included in the evaluations and in the reports on those evaluations.

The term *educational program* is a broad concept which includes several elements and which has vague parameters. A curriculum is one element of a program, teaching is another, and learning is a third. The support structure outside the classroom is a fourth. The interdependence of each element with another within each program, and the interdependence of each element with its kind in another program make the parameters of a given program truly ambiguous. The mathematics curriculum at one grade level, for example, is interconnected with the teaching and learning of mathematics in another grade level as well as with the support structure which the school provides for the mathematics program in other grade levels. At the same time, the mathematics curriculum in one grade level is interconnected with the mathematics curriculum in another grade level. The same teacher may teach mathematics in several grade levels in the secondary school or may teach arithmetic and other subject matters in the same classroom in the elementary school. The students learn mathematics and other subject matter simultaneously. And the support structure which the school provides for the mathematics program in one grade level is usually in accord with the support structure it provides for the mathematics program in another grade level or for other programs in the same grade level.

Because of the complicated nature of a given educational program, it is extremely difficult to conceptualize its relationship to levels of student achievement. Ironically, for this same reason teachers are more apt to accept evaluation of educational programs, even if the evaluation employs data on student achievement and its results imply failure. Since the program boundaries are ambiguous, the connections between the boundaries and levels of student achievement are ambiguous, and it is extremely difficult to identify anyone in particular who is responsible for the failure. If the evaluation implies success, then many can claim credit for it and can be justified in their claim.

School leaders may exercise relatively wide discretionary powers in their use of student achievement data to evaluate programs. They may use it to evaluate the curriculum, the teaching, the learning, and the support structure, rather than with only one specific activity, such as developing instructional objectives. There is an irony here, too. The very breadth of this power makes its impact on levels of student achievement highly indirect and unclear.

School principals are aware of the ambiguity of program boundaries. They are also aware of their wide discretionary powers in using student achievement data to evaluate educational programs, as well as the ambiguous impact of such use on student achievement. The first purpose of this study was to examine how strongly they believed in the assumptions associated with this use of the data and how extensively they reported its use. Accordingly, they were asked the following questions:

(1) To what extent do you believe that you should use data on student achievement to evaluate most educational programs in your school?

(2) To what extent do you believe that your use of the data on student achievement is an effective way to evaluate most educational programs in your school?

(3) To what extent do you believe that your use of the data on student achievement in evaluating most educational programs in your school has a positive effect on (a) most programs? (b) student achievement in most programs?

(4) To what extent do you use data on student achievement to evaluate (a) most educational programs in your school? (b) programs in which most of your teachers, students, or grade levels are involved? (c) programs in which most classes perform above school expectations? (d) programs in which most classes perform below school expectations?

Demands for educational accountability have resulted not only in program evaluation but also in evaluation reports transmitted to individuals, groups, or agencies outside the school. It is unclear whether student achievement data need to be included in these reports because of the multiple ways in which external agencies may use the reports. The second purpose of the study, therefore, was to examine how strongly principals felt they should include the data in their evaluation reports and how extensively they do include the data. Principals were asked two questions in this regard:

(5) To what extent do you believe that you should report data on student achievement in your evaluations of most educational programs in your school?

(6) To what extent do you report data on student achievement in your evaluations of most educational programs in your school?

A great many elements in a given educational program may promote controversy. For example, the specific content of a program or a specific teaching method may be controversial. Such elements may be specific to certain persons and not necessarily widespread in the school district, even though the educational program is used in the entire district. These elements may also be rooted in the personal philosophies and values of individual teachers. School principals are usually aware of the existence of such elements, and sometimes they tolerate them. Sometimes these elements exist because of the principal's own views.

Principals take the controversial nature of such elements into account when they evaluate a program. In their reports, however, they may not be able to defend the controversial elements if the recipients of the report do not approve of those elements. In such cases, the use of student achievement data in the evaluation report may not help resolve value-laden issues. The extent to which principals should use such data in reporting on controversial programs is therefore an important question. The third purpose of this study was to examine this concern. Two additional questions were asked:

(7) To what extent do you believe that data on student achievement should be emphasized when reporting evaluations of educational programs in your school (a) whose content is controversial? (b) which employ controversial teaching methods?

(8) To what extent do you emphasize data on student achievement when reporting evaluations of educational programs in your school (a) whose content is controversial? (b) which employ controversial teaching methods?

The study therefore sought to examine three sets of assumptions about student achievement data-based program evaluation and reporting, as well as whether principals acted on those assumptions. How strongly principals believed in the assumptions was examined by asking how they felt about the use of such data in evaluations (questions 1, 2, and 3), whether the data should be included in evaluation reports (question 5), and whether the data should be emphasized in reports of evaluation of controversial programs (question 7). How much the data was actually used was examined in the corresponding three areas (questions 4, 6, and 8).

Responses

Each of the questions had a 7-point rating scale. The means and standard deviations of responses are displayed in table 9.1 for each of the questions and for both groups of principals.

As table 9.1 shows, all the means are above the midpoint on the response scale. The highest means occur for the first two sets of assumptions and the first two sets of uses (questions 1–6). Principals felt strongest about questions 1 and 5: the need to use student achievement data in evaluating programs and the need to include the data in evaluation reports. They reported to have used data most extensively in reports of evaluations (question 6).

The table also shows relatively low means for both groups of principals on the third set of assumptions and the third set of uses (questions 7 and 8). Some principals in both groups responded below the midpoint on the scale. The number of these incidences was large, as can be surmised from the relatively large size of the corresponding standard deviations associated with the four means in each group of principals. These relatively lower means reflect a relatively weaker belief that student achievement data should be emphasized in reports of evaluation of controversial programs, as well as a relatively lower emphasis on this use..

The relatively lower positive means on questions 7 and 8 prompted the hypotheses that (a) principals are especially hesitant about emphasizing student achievement data when reporting evaluations of controversial programs; and that (b) principals actually emphasize the data less when reporting evaluation of controversial programs than they do in using the data in their evaluations and including the data in their reports on most programs.

These hypotheses were then tested. The responses to each of the questions for each group of principals were standardized in four groups of questions. Group 1 contained question 7; group 2 contained questions 1, 2, 3, and 5; group 3 contained question 8; and group 4 contained questions 4 and 6. T-tests were applied separately for each group of principals between group 1 and group 2 and between group 3 and group 4. A ≤ 0.05 level of significance was adopted. Confidence intervals were calculated to confirm the levels of significance. In both groups of principals, the differences between question groups 1 and 2 and between question groups 3 and 4 were significant.

In both groups of principals, the confidence in emphasizing student achievement data in reports on evaluation of controversial programs was significantly lower than that in all other assumptions combined. The reported extent of such emphasis was also significantly lower than that of all other uses combined. Because the differences were found to be significant for both groups of principals, it is highly probable that they exist in the minds of all elementary school principals in California in elementary school districts.

Table 9.1 Responses of Principals to Questions Concerning the Use of Student Achievement Data in Program Evaluation

| Question group | Question | Response (1 = low; 7 = high) | | | |
| | | Group 1[a] | | Group 2[b] | |
		Mean	Standard deviation	Mean	Standard deviation
Assumptions about use of student achievement data	1. Should you use student achievement data to evaluate most educational programs?	5.64	0.96	5.41	1.09
	2. Is your use of those data an effective way to evaluate programs?	5.50	0.93	5.27	1.04
	3a. Does your use of those data have a positive effect on most programs?	5.50	0.92	5.32	0.92
	3b. Does your use of those data have a positive effect on student achievement?	5.45	0.99	5.33	0.92
	5. Should you report those data in your evaluations of most programs?	5.62	0.99	5.38	1.10
	7a. Should you emphasize those data when reporting evaluations of programs whose content is controversial?	4.76	1.57	4.37	1.45
	7b. Should you emphasize those data when reporting evaluations of programs which employ controversial teaching methods?	5.09	1.41	4.55	1.49
Extent of use of student achievement data	4a. Do you use student achievement data in evaluating most programs?	5.45	1.05	5.22	1.22
	4b. Do you use those data in evaluating programs which involve most of your teachers, students, or grade levels?	5.58	0.98	5.38	1.06
	4c. Do you use those data in evaluating programs in which most classes perform above school expectations?	5.45	1.15	5.32	1.18

Table 9.1 Responses of Principals to Questions Concerning the Use of Student Achievement Data in Program Evaluation *(continued)*

| Question group | Question | Response (1 = low; 7 = high) | | | |
| | | Group 1[a] | | Group 2[b] | |
		Mean	Standard deviation	Mean	Standard deviation
Extent of use of student achievement data	4d. Do you use those data in evaluating programs in which most classes perform below school expectations?	5.56	1.08	5.35	1.17
	6. Do you report those data in your evaluations of most programs?	5.66	0.96	5.57	1.04
	8a. Do you emphasize those data when reporting evaluations of programs whose content is controversial?	4.58	1.49	4.60	1.41
	8b. Do you emphasize those data when reporting evaluations of programs which employ controversial teaching methods?	4.83	1.45	4.75	1.45

[a] Principals nominated by supervisors as "most effective" (174 principals).
[b] Principals nominated by supervisors as "least effective" (97 principals).

Analysis

Some of the data indicate that principals believe more strongly in the need to use student achievement data in program evaluation (question 1) and in the need to include such data in their evaluation reports (question 5) than in the value of this use (questions 2 and 3). The stronger belief in the *need* may be associated with demands for accountability. The somewhat less strong belief in the *value* may be associated with the unclear, indirect, and, at best, distant influence of program evaluation and reporting on actual student achievement. How else can one interpret the finding that data on student achievement were used more in evaluation reports (question 6) than in evaluation itself (question 4) by both groups of principals and regardless of levels of class performance (question 4, c and d)?

The significantly lower means for both groups of principals on questions 7 and 8 than on all other items reflect the caution with which principals emphasize student achievement data in reporting their evaluation of controversial programs. They probably suspect that the data may not be as useful as it might be in reporting on noncontroversial programs. Moreover, principals do not believe strongly in the need to use the data, nor do they report a high extent of such use. The means on questions 7 and 8 were found to be highly correlated, as can be seen in tables 9.2 and 9.3 for both groups of principals. These two tables were constructed on the basis of the Pearson's product moment test statistic, which was used to compute correlations among all 14 questions for the two groups of principals separately.

Small ranges were detected between the two groups of principals for the questions on how much principals used student achievement data in program evaluation (question 4). This finding may reflect a uniform response to demands for accountability in program evaluation. Small ranges were also detected for questions on principals' confidence in the effect of such data on programs (question 3a) and on student achievement (question 3b). It may be that a uniform level of understanding exists among principals about the value of using such data for either formative outcomes (programs) or summative outcomes (student achievement). This understanding may be influenced by the requirement to use the data as well as by the principals' independent judgment about the value of its use.

Table 9.2 Interitem Correlations of Responses by 174 "Most Effective" Principals to Questions Concerning the Use of Student Achievement Data in Program Evaluation

Question	2	3a	3b	5	7a	7b	4a	4b	4c	4d	6	8a	8b
1	.59	.47	.49	.73	.44	.48	.52	.54	.15	.31	.34	.22	.31
2		.49	.36	.60	.43	.49	.53	.58	.35	.44	.46	.32	.36
3a			.46	.21	.31	.43	.60	.43	.21	.31	.45	.61	.50
3b				.36	.12	.25	.34	.51	.28	.46	.48	.29	.27
5					.44	.44	.49	.54	.19	.41	.45	.22	.26
7a						.80	.29	.29	.17	.16	.30	.69	.54
7b							.31	.34	.18	.23	.33	.63	.74
4a								.74	.45	.42	.61	.32	.35
4b									.44	.53	.57	.31	.38
4c										.61	.46	.30	.27
4d											.42	.16	.22
6												.36	.35
8a													.84

The ranges between the two groups of principals were wider on the rest of the questions which reflect strength of beliefs in assumptions (see table 9.4). The differences between the two groups on questions 1, 5, and 2 were significant at the ≤ 0.09 level when a t-test was computed. The differences on question 7a was significant at the 0.045 level and on question 7b at the 0.004 level.

These five differences probably suggest that there is no uniformity in principals' beliefs about emphasizing the data when reporting evaluation of controversial programs (question 7), about the value of the data in evaluations (question 2), about the need to include the data in reports (question 5), and about the need to use the data in evaluation (question 1). It may be that many principals are simply uncertain about the use of student achievement data in evaluations and in evaluation

Table 9.3   Interitem Correlations of Responses by 97 "Least Effective" Principals to Questions Concerning the Use of Student Achievement Data in Program Evaluation

Question	2	3a	3b	5	7a	7b	4a	4b	4c	4d	6	8a	8b
1	.61	.32	.23	.85	.42	.39	.52	.41	.39	.45	.42	.31	.29
2		.19	.55	.60	.36	.42	.41	.37	.55	.54	.35	.27	.33
3a			.16	.38	.46	.42	.28	.50	.37	.38	.15	.12	.32
3b				.17	.24	.37	.43	.51	.34	.51	.62	.21	.43
5					.36	.34	.47	.36	.34	.43	.35	.22	.25
7a						.87	.50	.31	.15	.19	.22	.74	.67
7b							.43	.33	.23	.27	.26	.68	.66
4a								.65	.43	.52	.55	.48	.52
4b									.47	.52	.65	.41	.44
4c										.73	.46	.29	.28
4d											.52	.29	.33
6												.38	.38
8a													.91

reporting. Some principals may feel that their discretionary powers to use the data are wide. Others may not. Many of them may be uncertain about the impact of this data on student achievement. It may be that individual principals have private opinions on the subject. It may also be that individual principals value the opinions of others differently. Principals' private opinions may heavily dictate what they in fact do with the data in evaluating programs and reporting on those evaluations.

Table 9.4 Differences between Mean Responses of Principals to Questions 7, 2, 5, and 1

Question	Mean of group 1[a]	Mean of group 2[b]	t	P
7b. Should you emphasize student achievement data when reporting evaluations of programs whose content is controversial?	5.09	4.55	2.86	0.004
7a. Should you emphasize those data when reporting evaluations of programs which employ controversial teaching methods?	4.76	4.37	2.02	0.045
2. Is your use of the data an effective way to evaluate most programs?	5.50	5.27	1.80	(0.075)
5. Should you report those data in your evaluations of most programs?	5.62	5.38	1.75	(0.083)
1. Should you use those data to evaluate most programs?	5.64	5.41	1.72	(0.088)

Note: Scale is 1 to 7, where 1 = low and 7 = high.

[a] Principals nominated by supervisors as "most effective" (174 principals).

[b] Principals nominated by supervisors as "least effective" (97 principals).

Chapter 10

School Leadership and Interaction with Teachers

Questions

Demands for educational accountability have focused on the use of student achievement data to measure school quality. Since teacher quality is central to school quality, one of the central responsibilities of a school leader is to guide and inspire teachers. The most fundamental way that principals can respond to demands for higher quality is to share student achievement data with their teachers. The assumption here is that only if teachers are made aware of the data are they likely to incorporate them into their teaching. The first purpose of this study was to examine how strongly principals believed in this assumption, as well as how extensively they actually shared the data. They were asked two questions in this regard:

(1) To what extent do you believe that sharing data on student achievement with individual teachers has a positive effect on student achievement?

(2) To what extent do you share data on student achievement with most teachers in your school?

Evaluation mandates have required that teachers be evaluated on the basis of student achievement. While this exercise is an important part of school leaders' interaction with their teachers, it is also problematic. It was seen in chapter 7 that arguments both for and against evaluating teachers on the basis of student achievement have merit. Teachers and principals may be unclear as to the exact purpose of this evaluation, whether it is essentially symbolic or substantive in nature. A *symbolic* interpretation dictates that student achievement data which pertain to specific teachers be collected and at least reported. In so doing, schools would give the impression that they evaluate teachers on the basis of those data, even if they do not actually make decisions on the basis of their evaluations. School district bureaucracies are interested in creating this impression so that they appear to be responding to demands for accountability. A *substantive* interpretation dictates that student achievement data which pertain to specific teachers be collected and analyzed along with other data to assess the performance of teachers and to suggest adjustments in classroom teaching. These activities may or may not produce demonstrable results. They are also time consuming and somewhat threatening to teachers who do not believe that the purpose is solely substantive. But they do have the potential to improve student performance.

Principals have difficulty engaging in activities which are designed to fulfill both purposes simultaneously. If they do engage in both, they probably need to use a separate set of data for each purpose (Glasman 1974, 1977). They also need to convince teachers that they (the principals) are required to fulfill both purposes (Glasman and Paulin 1982). It may be unwise for principals to publicize this two-pronged engagement in evaluation. Principals are aware of their dilemma. If they engage in both sets of activities, then the "private" dimension of their leadership may become public and cause them to lose credibility with outsiders. If they engage only in substantive evaluation, then their central district office may think they are disloyal. If they engage only in symbolic evaluation, their teachers may think they lack authority.

The second purpose of this study was to examine principals' perceptions about their dilemma. Three questions were asked:

(3) To what extent do you believe that data on student achievement should be used in evaluating teachers?

(4) To what extent do you use data on student achievement in evaluating teachers whose classes perform (a) above school expectations? (b) below school expectations?

(5) To what extent do you believe that your use of data on student achievement to evaluate teachers is an effective way to

(a) reinforce teachers' use of effective instructional techniques or curricula? (b) modify teachers' use of instructional techniques or curricula? (c) control teachers' use of instructional techniques or curricula? (d) limit the between-teacher variation in the use of instructional techniques or curricula?

All three sets of questions dealt with the substantive purpose of teacher evaluation, although the first two sets were sufficiently general to permit principals to consider the symbolic purpose as well.

Responses

A 7-point rating scale was used to measure responses. The means and standard deviations of responses are displayed in table 10.1 for each of the questions and for both groups of principals.

As this table shows, all the means are above the midpoint on the response scale. The highest mean is for the reported sharing of data on student achievement with teachers (question 2), and the next highest is for the belief that sharing the data has a positive effect on student achievement (question 1). The table also shows relatively low means for both groups of principals on the belief that using student achievement data to evaluate teachers is an effective way to control (question 5c) or limit (question 5d) variations in instructional techniques or curriculum. The mean for group 2 was also relatively low regarding the belief that data on student achievement should be used to evaluate teachers (question 3). In all five instances (questions 1, 2, 3, 5c and 5d), the relatively large standard deviations suggest that a large number of principals responded below the midpoint on the scale.

The relatively lower positive means on questions 5c and 5d for both groups of principals prompted the hypothesis that principals may have significantly less confidence that using data to evaluate teachers is an effective way to control teachers' classroom behavior or limit variation of this behavior than they do in the rest of their beliefs (questions 1, 3, 5a, and 5b). The hypothesis was tested by applying t-tests between questions 5c and each of the questions 1, 3, 5a, and 5b separately for each group of principals, and by applying t-tests between question 5d and each of the other four questions for each group of principals.

Table 10.1 Responses of Principals to Questions Concerning the Use of Student Achievement Data in Interactions with Teachers

| | Response (1 = low; 7 = high) | | | |
| | Group 1[a] | | Group 2[b] | |
Question	Mean	Standard deviation	Mean	Standard deviation
1. Does sharing student achievement data with individual teachers have a positive effect on student achievement?	5.76	0.97	5.47	1.14
2. Do you share those data with most teachers?	6.14	0.98	6.07	1.02
3. Should those data be used in evaluating teachers?	5.30	1.27	4.78	1.50
4a. Do you use those data to evaluate teachers whose classes perform above school expectations?	5.10	1.62	5.31	1.40
4b. Do you use those data to evaluate teachers whose classes perform below school expectations?	5.16	1.57	5.23	1.49
5a. Is your use of those data to evaluate teachers an effective way to reinforce their use of instructional techniques or curricula?	5.36	1.45	5.26	1.38
5b. Is your use of those data to evaluate teachers an effective way to modify their use of instructional techniques or curricula?	5.13	1.43	5.02	1.33
5c. Is your use of those data to evaluate teachers an effective way to control their use of instructional techniques or curricula?	4.66	1.40	4.70	1.29
5d. Is your use of those data to evaluate teachers an effective way to limit the between-teacher variation in the use of instructional techniques or curricula?	4.08	1.16	4.41	1.33

[a] Principals nominated by supervisors as "most effective" (174 principals).
[b] Principals nominated by supervisors as "least effective" (97 principals).

The differences between question 5c and the others were not significant. The differences between question 5d and the others were significant only for the 5d-1 and 5d-3 pairs and only for group 1. Thus, at least for some principals in the sample, confidence in the effectiveness of using outcome data to evaluate teachers and thereby limit the variation in classroom behaviors is significantly lower than confidence in either the positive effect of sharing the data with teachers on student achievement or in the need to use the data to evaluate teachers.

The relatively lower positive means on questions 5c and 5d for each group of principals also prompted the hypothesis that principals' belief in either item is significantly lower than their reported actions. More specifically, the means of either questions 5c or 5d were hypothesized as significantly lower than for each of questions 2, 4a, and 4b. The application of t-tests here produced a significant difference for both groups of principals between question 5d and question 2. In both groups, principals' confidence in the effectiveness of using outcome data to evaluate teachers and thereby limit the variation in classroom behaviors was found to be significantly lower than their reported use of the data to evaluate teachers. Given the findings in both groups of principals, it is highly probable that they exist in the minds of all elementary school principals in California who are employed in elementary school districts.

Analysis

The relatively high means for both groups of principals on question 2 should come as no surprise. To share student achievement data with teachers is the least principals can do when they are called upon to exercise accountability. This act alone, however, does not necessarily guide or inspire teachers to use the data to improve their teaching. It may tell teachers that the principal attaches a high value to this kind of data. But it is still uncertain whether sharing those data indicates that principals are confident that this sharing will improve student achievement, even though this belief was also found to be relatively strong (question 1).

The means for both groups of principals on questions 3 and 4 were lower than for those on questions 1 and 2. The former group questioned whether student achievement data should be used to evaluate teachers (question 3) and the extent to which principals reported that they use the data to evaluate teachers (questions 3 and 4). It may be that using the data to evaluate teachers is simply not as common as sharing the data with teachers. This conjecture is supported by nation-wide data generated in 1982. In that study, both principals and teachers reported that principals take test scores into account when they evaluate teachers significantly less frequently than they meet with teachers to review the scores (Dorr-Bremme 1983). If true, this possibility has nothing to do with the level of student performance as measured by class aggregates (questions 4a and 4b had similar means). Rather, it may have to do with the more complex notion of evaluating teachers as compared to sharing data with them for some other purpose.

The uncertainty surrounding the dilemma associated with the symbolic and the substantive nature of evaluating teachers on the basis of student achievement data may contribute to a lack of uniform response among principals. This lack of uniformity is clearly indicated by the large range of responses to question 3: how strongly principals believe such data should be used in evaluation. The t-test which was used here revealed a difference ($t=2.87$) which was significant at the 0.005 level.

The lack of uniformity among principals extends even to question 1: the belief that sharing student achievement data with teachers has a positive effect on student achievement. The t-test which was used here revealed a difference ($t=2.03$) which was significant at the 0.05 level. It may be that the symbolic versus substantive dilemma has permeated the interaction of principals with teachers even when the data on student achievement are only shared and not explicitly associated with teacher evaluation.

Principals' beliefs in the substantive teaching benefits of using out-come data in teacher evaluation (question 5) turned out to be no stronger, and in some cases (questions 5c and 5d) weaker, than the more general belief in using the data to evaluate teachers (question 3). In fact, the lowest means for both groups of principals turned out to be on questions which dealt with controlling teachers' activities in the classroom (question 5c) and with limiting variations among teachers (question 5d). These questions reflect more coercive adjustment in classroom behavior than do questions 5a and 5b.

Principals' inability or lack of interest in coercing teachers to change their classroom behavior may be unassociated with their general use of student achievement data. A Gamma test statistic was used to compute interitem correlations for each group of principals separately. The test was made to determine possible reasons for the low means on questions 5c and 5d. It was reasoned that the fewer low correlations there are between questions 5c and 5d and each of the rest of the items in this study, the more likely it is that there is randomness of interitem differences, and therefore, perhaps, no differentiation in the minds of principals between reasons for their beliefs in questions 5c and 5d and in other questions. The interitem correlations are displayed in table 10.2 for the first group of principals, and in table 10.3 for the second group.

Table 10.2 Interitem Correlations of Responses by 174 "Most Effective" Principals to Questions Concerning the Use of Student Achievement Data in Interactions with Teachers

Question	2	3	4a	4b	5a	5b	5c	5d
1	.542	.625	.442	.462	.538	.495	.343	.164
2		.306	.551	.455	.510	.522	.418	.225
3			.575	.534	.534	.447	.267	.206
4a				.807	.662	.681	.551	.354
4b					.652	.662	.570	.355
5a						.832	.610	.421
5b							.721	.462
5c								.633

For the purposes of these considerations, it may be assumed that a magnitude of <0.300 reflects randomness on a given interitem difference, and that a magnitude of <0.300 reflects no randomness. As it turned out, a great majority of the correlations between questions 5c or 5d and any other question had a magnitude of ≥ 0.300. The one exception was with question 3 in the first group of principals. The magnitude of the correlation was 0.267, but it was not significant at a sufficiently low probability. There were some exceptions in the correlations between question 5d and others. In the first group of principals, the correlation between questions 5d and 1 was 0.164 at

Table 10.3   Interitem Correlations of Responses by 97 "Least Effective" Principals to Questions Concerning the Use of Student Achievement Data in Interactions with Teachers

Question	2	3	4a	4b	5a	5b	5c	5d
1	.590	.574	.411	.406	.532	.595	.638	.427
2		.196	.467	.475	.394	.424	.565	.390
3			.395	.490	.451	.526	.368	.293
4a				.863	.623	.552	.449	.319
4b					.526	.635	.502	.353
5a						.749	.680	.473
5b							.664	.490
5c								.769

p =0.11; the correlation between questions 5d and 2 was 0.225 at 0.002 < p <0.02; and the correlation between questions 5d and 3 was 0.206 at p <0.002. In the second group of principals, the correlation between questions 5d and 3 was 0.293 at p =0.09.

In the second group of principals, then, there are no interitem correlations which are small at a sufficiently low probability level. Interitem differences may be random, and principals' reasons for responding to questions 5c and 5d in the way they did may have nothing to do with the focus on student achievement data. The low means on questions 5c and 5d may have more to do with their view of teachers as semiautonomous professionals whose discretionary powers in the classroom are to be reckoned with and respected.

For the first group of principals, the only two interitem correlations which are small at a sufficiently low probability level are between question 5d and questions 2 and 3. Question 2 deals with the reported sharing of student achievement data with teachers. Question 3 deals with the belief that the data should be used to evaluate teachers. Here, perhaps, there are additional reasons for the significantly lower belief in the effectiveness of limiting variation in the classroom by using student achievement data to evaluate teachers. One reason may be associated with collective bargaining contracts, which prohibit this use of data.

The findings in this study tell us several things about the interaction between school leaders and teachers regarding student achievement. First, principals strongly believe that sharing data with teachers may have a positive effect on student achievement. Second, many principals do share data with teachers. Third, principals believe that data on student achievement should be used to evaluate teachers, perhaps more formatively than summatively. Fourth, many principals actually use those data to evaluate teachers. And finally, they do not believe that such data can be used effectively to coerce teachers to change their teaching habits.

Chapter *11*

School Leadership and
Student Achievement Problems

Questions

Although schools are not often characterized by their problems, school leadership is often characterized by problem solving. School principals spend a considerable proportion of their time solving or attempting to solve difficult situations. The demands for educational accountability have obviously made them give particular attention to problems associated with student achievement.

This study sought to concentrate on problems associated with student achievement and specifically on principals' involvement with those problems. Since student achievement problems existed before demands for educational accountability intensified, this study did not focus on responses to those demands. District guidelines for solving student achievement problems may have existed before demands increased, and there may have been some recent adjustments in those guidelines. But neither external evaluation mandates not districtwide guidelines specify in sufficient detail the frequency and the manner in which school principals need to solve or attempt to solve problems associated with student achievement. Neither do mandates and guidelines sufficiently specify when and how principals need to report on their problem-solving attempts.

School principals' involvement in achievement problems varies, to a large extent, by school and by principal. Obviously, how a school leader handles achievement problems has a much more direct bearing on student performance than many other aspects of school leadership. The principal handles these problems as directly as his or her authority permits and as he or she chooses within the context of that authority.

This study sought to examine principals' involvement only with problems associated with low achievers. Two fundamental elements of that involvement can be derived from the pertinent literature (e.g., California State Department of Education 1977; Brookover et al. 1978; Wellisch et al. 1978; Berman and McLaughlin 1979; Venezky and Winfield 1979; Leithwood and Montgomery 1982). One element is the proactive nature of the involvement. The other is the strength of the involvement.

Proactivity relates to the energy with which principals take the initiative to become involved in a problem. First they must become aware of the problem's existence; at this point, they experience the problem and initiate attempts to handle it. The more they experience a problem and become so involved, the more proactive they are. The *strength* of the involvement is then determined by the actions taken to solve the problem — specifically, by their scope and substance. *Scope* implies the range of involvement, or how many different actions are taken. *Substance* implies the depth of involvement, or how much detail and clarity the activities have. The specific purposes of this study were therefore to examine the following:

(1) how often principals' experience common problems associated with low-achieving students;

(2) how often principals actively participate in the problem-solving process;

(3) the scope of principals' involvement in the problem-solving process; and

(4) the substance of principals' involvement in the problem-solving process.

The following steps were taken to address the first purpose of the study. A pilot study was conducted in central California to identify the most common academic problems of low achieving students in elementary schools. Seven problems were found to occur most frequently:

(1) Principals discover low spelling scores in one classroom.

(2) Principals discover that the third grade level's California Assessment Program (CAP) punctuation scores have been low for three years.

(3) Principals discover that California Assessment Program (CAP) scores as measured by data on grades 3 and 6 are low compared to scores from other schools.

(4) A teacher requests help with one low-achieving student.

(5) All fourth grade teachers complain about the third grade mathematics scores of their incoming students and ask for help.

(6) All first grade teachers ask for help with immaturity-related reading problems with many of their students.

(7) The district office requests that efforts be made to improve the performance of low-achieving students in the school.

All principals in the survey population were given these seven typical problems and asked to indicate whether they had experienced them. In three of these situations, principals became aware of the problem and initiated attempts to handle it before anyone else requested them to do so (problems 1, 2, and 3). One of these typically dealt with the performance of an entire classroom, another with an entire grade level, and a third with an entire school. In three other situations (problems 4, 5, and 6), the problem was brought to the principal's attention by teachers. One of these typically dealt with one low-achieving students, and the other two with an entire grade level. The seventh problem was usually first brought to the principal's attention by the district school office and dealt with general achievement scores in the entire school.

The second, third, and fourth purposes of the study were fulfilled in the following way. Principals in the survey population were asked to select one of the 7 problems and to describe what they had done to solve it. They were not asked to indicate the success of their involvement, only to describe each of their actions with as much detail, clarity, and specificity as they could. Their responses were seen as reflecting either active or passive participation. The use of the active voice was seen to indicate active participation; the use of the passive voice, passive participation. The number of described actions was used to represent the scope of the involvement, and the number of detailed, clear, and specific descriptions of actions was used to represent the substance of the involvement.

Responses

A smaller number of responses was used in this study than in the previous three studies because the response return was smaller. In the first group of principals, only 144 usable questionnaires were returned, or 83 percent of the 93 percent return rate in the other studies. In the second group of principals, only 71 usable questionnaires were returned, or 73 percent of the 83 percent return rate in the other studies. Table 11.1 displays the percentage of principals in each group who indicated that they had experienced any of the seven problems.

Table 11.1   Principals' Experience with Low Performance Scores

Problem number	Subject area	Number of Low-achievers	Source of principal's awareness	Percentage of principals who reported having experienced the problem	
				Group 1[a]	Group 2[b]
1	Spelling	One classroom	Principal	65	67
2	Punctuation	One grade level	Principal	31	40
3	General	Entire school	Principal	32	33
4	General	One student	Teachers	98	98
5	Mathematics	One grade level	Teachers	61	64
6	Reading	One grade level	Teachers	52	64
7	General	Entire school	District office	29	37

[a] Principals nominated by supervisors as "most effective" (144 principals).
[b] Principals nominated by supervisors as "least effective" (71 principals).

About two-thirds of both groups of principals reported having experienced problem 1, and about one-third of both groups of principals reported having experienced problems 2 and 3. Almost all principals in both groups reported having experienced problem 4; between one-third and one-half in both groups, problems 5 and 6; and about one-third in both groups, problem 7.

No attempt was made to analyze the content of the response to the open-ended question by problem number. Thus the second, third, and fourth purposes of the study were pursued without regard to any particular situation. In the first group of principals, 74 percent were classified as "more active than passive" participants and 26 percent as "more passive than active." In the second group, the corresponding percentages were 46 and 54. The difference between the two groups of principals was statistically significant (x $=$ 10.46; p $=$ .0.01) and thus reflected a large range of responses. The means for the number of mentioned actions (signifying the scope of the activity) were 12.67 for group 1 and 10.53 for group 2. The difference between these means was not statistically significant (t $=$ 1.65; p $=$ 0.20). The means for the number of specifically described actions (signifying the substance of the activity) were 13.18 for the first group of principals (equal variation; t $=$ 2.02; df $=$ 179.5; p $=$ 0.04) and 10.44 for the second group of principals (unequal variation; t $=$ *1.64;* df $=$ 183.0; p $=$ 0.10). The difference between these means was statistically significant, indicating a large range of response.

Analysis

Several reasons may be advanced for the interitem differences in the percentage of principals who experienced a specific typical problem. One explanation may lie in how often the problem occurred. Another may be in the number of subjects who actually experienced the problem. A third may relate to who first became aware of the problem: the principal or someone else. Since each of these explanations may be relevant to some situations but not to others, none of them is sufficient by itself.

The actual frequency by which a problem occurs may depend on the number of cases which come up. A problem with an individual student may occur more frequently than a problem with a whole classroom because there are more students than classrooms in a given school. Likewise, a problem with a classroom may occur more frequently than a problem with a grade level, and the latter more frequently than one with an entire school. Thus, for example, problem 4, which deals with individual students, is reported as having been experienced by 98 percent of the principals, and problem 2, 5, and 6, which deal with classrooms, is reported as having been experienced by smaller percentages of principals. Problem 1, which deals with one classroom, is reported as having been experienced by more principals than problem 2, which deals with one grade level. But this line of reasoning does not explain, for example, the higher percentage with regard to problem 5, which deals with a grade level, than that with regard to problem 2, which also deals with a grade level.

The number of subjects which, in fact, experience the problem may depend on the number of specific skills in which students' scores are low. A problem with one skill may occur more frequently than a problem with several skills at once. Thus, for example, problem 1, dealing with spelling, is reported as having been experienced by 66 percent of the principals, while problems 3 and 7, dealing with general skills, by only about 33 percent. But this line of reasoning does not explain, for example, the higher percentage with regard to problem 6, reading, than that with regard to problem 2, punctuation, both of which constitute only one type of skill.

Who first becomes aware of a problem may also influence how frequently the problem occurs. Others may bring problems to principals' attention much more frequently than principals may seek to identify problems themselves. Thus, in problems 2, 5, and 6, the frequency of occurrence as well as the number of subject skills in which the problem exists are both identical, but problems 5 and 6 are reported to have been experienced by significantly more principals than problem 2 — perhaps because in problems 5 and 6 teachers bring the problems to the principal, while in problem 2 the principal acts first. This line of argument, however, does not explain the similarity in percentages between problem 7, where the district office brings the problem to the attention of the principal, and problems 2 and 3, where the principal seeks to identify the problem. Nonetheless, the reactive nature of the principal's experience with the problem may serve as a central explanation for iteritem differences, because there are many more teachers than school district officers who can bring a problem to the attention of the principal.

All of the above has dealt only with how frequently principals experience common achievement problems. The findings associated with the last three purposes of the study are also revealing. With regard to the active participation of principals in the problem-solving process, the range among the two groups of principals was large: 74 percent and 46 percent. It may be that most principals are more "reactive" than "proactive" in their awareness of problems but vary widely in their involvement in the problem-solving process.

Regarding the strength of principals' involvement — the number of actions mentioned and the number of detailed descriptions of these actions — principals seem to be highly active. To report over 10 actions taken personally and to describe over 10 detailed instances of personal actions is to reveal a highly intense involvement. Clearly, so many actions described in detail cannot be invented unless they had in fact occurred. It is true that these responses described occurrences of the past. Perhaps such language should be examined also from a more psycholinguistic point of view, since it tended to be quite descriptive. In some cases, principals wrote as many as 1,000 words, despite the fact that the open-ended question was the last one to be asked in the entire California study.

The entire set of responses to this open-ended question is reported elsewhere (Patterson 1984). A close examination of the content of those responses reveals a multitude of highly specific, clear, and detailed descriptions of a variety of personal actions. Among them are suggestions made to teachers about diagnoses and remedies, provisions for supporting teachers, revisions on both these suggestions, and suggestions for monitoring teachers' progress and student responses. These responses include detailed descriptions of what school leadership may be in dealing with data-based problems associated with low-achieving students. They constitute a rich source for learning more about administrative situations at the school level. Several writers have recently argued for the need to elicit more such descriptions (e.g., Griffiths 1979, p.58).

Chapter *12*

Student Achievement Data as an Administrative Resource: A Summary

Commitment to Improving Student Achievement

Can principals influence student achievement, and if so, how? The principals surveyed in the California study were found to have a relatively strong orientation toward student achievement (see the mean responses of the two groups to question 4 in table 8.1). The variation among principals with regard to their strong orientation was relatively small. Not only were the two means close, but the range of responses of the two groups of principals were only 0.82 and 0.92.

Principals also believed strongly in the four specific ways in which they could improve student achievement. They believed they could reduce student learning to specific instructional objectives, that they could influence teachers to teach to specific instructional objectives, that student achievement could be improved by teaching to those objectives, and that achievement data in turn influenced instructional objectives (see table 8.1, questions, 1, 2, 3, and 5). The variation among principals was relatively small except on question 2, where the responses of most principals ranged from 4 to 7. This is the only situation in which their control is not independent of what teachers actually do behind the classroom doors.

Control over the Use of Student Achievement Data

How much control do principals think they have over their use of data on student achievement? The answer to this question may determine the consequences, regardless of whether the perception is true or false. This question was examined in relation to the development of instructional objectives, and interaction with teachers — the former a highly specific subject, and the latter a very general subject. Principals were asked six questions in this regard. The first four dealt with formalizing achievement-based objectives; making the objectives specific; clarifying them to teachers; and measuring achievement as a function of the objectives (see table 8.1, questions 6–9). The last two dealt with beliefs about sharing achievement data with teachers and the actual sharing of data with teachers (see table 10.1, question 1 and 2).

Principals were found to have relatively strong beliefs in these six items. The responses were highest for the last question, on whether principals do share student achievement data with teachers. This activity would not consume much of the principal's time if it did not involve any discussion, and the study did not pursue that question. The simple act of sharing data, of course, may at least send the message that principals care about the data. But power to share data does not imply an equal amount of power over what teachers, in fact, do with the data. Ironically, the act of sharing the data with teachers, although highly significant in a symbolic way, is far removed from activities which actually determine levels of student achievement. Nonetheless, principals reported that they often shared student achievement data, and the variation in their responses was relatively small.

For the question whether principals believed that sharing data with teachers has a positive effect on student achievement, the means were somewhat lower but still positive (see table 10.1, question 1). These answers express a belief in the consequences of an activity rather than actual engagement in an activity. The variation in responses on this item was relatively large, probably because principals' perceived control over the consequences of sharing data with teachers is personally and individually determined.

All the means of responses on the other four items — those associated with formalization, specificity, clarity, and measurability of achievement data-based objectives — were relatively high and relatively similar (See table 8.1, questions 6–9). These items relate to specific, time-consuming activities which are more capable of actually affecting levels of student achievement than is data sharing. The high level of principals' control over these activities is probably supported by the district office. But this control does not, in and of itself, dictate what teachers do in the classroom.

Use of Student Achievement Data in Evaluation

How do principals perceive their use of data on student achievement in evaluation? The answer to this question may determine the decisions and actions they take on the basis of evaluation results, although the study did not pursue this question. It may also reflect compliance with mandates to evaluate more than the actual influence of student achievement data on principals' decisions and actions. The study did not examine this possibility either. What could be assumed, but is in need of further study, is that the more principals use evaluation data to guide their decisions and actions, the more that use may have an impact on student achievement.

This assumption was examined in two aspects of leadership: program and teacher evaluation. Eight questions were asked in regard to program evaluation (see table 9.1, questions 1–4) and three with respect to teacher evaluation (see table 10.1, questions 3 and 4). In each group some questions dealt with beliefs in assumptions and some with actual use of the data.

All means on the eight questions dealing with program evaluation were relatively high, although some were lower than the means reported earlier in this chapter. They were also relatively uniform. The similarity in responses to questions about reported use of the data in evaluating programs, regardless of the actual level of student achievement, probably indicates that this activity has been highly institutionalized, a notion that is reinforced by the similarity between responses on reported use of the data and those on belief in assumptions. It may be that the level of institutionalization has become so high that it dictates not only principals' activities but also attitudes. This possibility makes principals' decisions and actions which may result from such program evaluation extremely important areas of investigation.

The means of responses of the two groups of principals on the three questions dealing with teacher evaluation were somewhat lower, and, in the case of the assumption, also varied (see table 10.1, questions 3 and 4). Perhaps the use of achievement data has not become as strongly institutionalized in teacher evaluation as it has in program evaluation. The variation among principals on their belief in the need to use the data was high, while variation on their actual use of the data to evaluate teachers was not — and it was particularly low with regard to evaluating teachers in low-achieving classes. It seems that a measure of institutionalization in using achievement data to evaluate teachers does exist, but that schools have proceeded cautiously in deference to teachers' sensitivity. What remains to be examined is how and how much principals are guided by the results of their evaluation.

Effectiveness and Accountability

How effective do principals think they are in using student achievement data? How do they perceive the accountability associated with that use? The first question deals with the immediate effect on teachers, and the second question with the extent to which teachers and principals are held accountable. In a way, both questions reflect principals' perceptions about the results of using student achievement data.

The first question was examined in relation to teacher evaluation and the development of instructional objectives. The second question was examined in relation to only the development of instructional objectives. In the first case, five questions were asked (see table 10.1, questions 5a, 5b, 5c, 5d; and table 8.1, question 10), and in the second, two questions (table 8.1, questions 11 and 12).

All the means on all seven questions were generally lower than those on the other questions discussed so far. The variation among principals for any of the seven questions was relatively large and in some cases approached points below the midpoint in the response scale. The highest number of responses below the midpoint in the response scale was in the third, fourth and sixth items (table 10.1, questions 5c and d; and table 8.1, question 11). Common to all three items is the belief that principals cannot very effectively force teachers to use achievement data to guide instruction and that principals do not hold teachers accountable for that use to a very great extent. The relatively low strength of this belief and the relatively large variation

among principals perhaps indicate that principals have serious difficulty in influencing teachers to teach in specific ways and do not have
any common approach to dealing with those difficulties. The means of
responses to the principals' accountability (table 8.1, questions 11 and
12) were somewhat higher but still relatively low and varied.

The Specific Issue of Principals' Accountability

How extensively do principals think they are held accountable for
the use of student achievement data? This question was asked in more
detail in relation to program evaluation. The reports which principals
submit to their respective district offices generally include data on student achievement. The principals' opinion on this inclusion therefore
represents one measure of their views on accountability.

Six questions were asked in this regard. Three of them dealt with
how strongly principals believed in including the data in the evaluation
reports (see table 9.1, questions 5, 7a, and 7b), and three others with
whether they actually include the data (see table 9.1, questions 6, 8a,
and 8b). In each set, one question dealt with evaluations of most
programs (questions 5 and 6) and two questions with evaluations of
controversial programs (questions 7a, 7b, 8a, and 8b).

The responses of the two groups of principals on their belief in,
and on their actual inclusion of, the data in most programs were
generally high, and variation in those responses was relatively low. The
means of responses pertaining to controversial programs were considerably lower; and the variation relatively high. In all cases the
means reached points below the midpoint in the scale.

These results suggest that principals believe they are accountable
for evaluating most programs and that they are less accountable for
evaluating controversial programs, both in theory and in practice. With
regard to controversial programs, principals are probably partially
opposed to, or at least uncertain about the wisdom of, including
achievement data in evaluation reports. Perhaps principals recognize
that data of any kind, and especially outcome data, may not very useful
in evaluation reports of programs over which there are disagreements
rooted in different value stances.

Direct Involvement with Achievement Problems

To what extent are principals aware of problem situations associated with low achievers? How directly are they involved in solving those problems? In this area, their use of achievement data would reflect directly on their leadership, and their commitment would imply a commitment to practice. Principals' control over the use of data is very high. They can conduct varied and extensive evaluations, and they may be very effective in enhancing student achievement. Finally, principals' accountability in this area is of more concern to principals themselves than it is to teachers or district officials. When principals help solve achievement problems of students, they make classroom and school management easier, and they probably also derive satisfaction from their actions themselves.

These two questions were examined by presenting seven common problem situations to principals (see table 11.1). A large majority reported having experienced some of these situations, and a large minority reported having experienced others.

Principals were also asked to choose one problem situation and to describe what they did to solve it. Their reports were analyzed as reflecting more active or more passive behavior, and variation on this criterion was wide. The variations on two other criteria — the number of reported actions taken by the principal and the number of clearly and specifically described actions — were also wide. On the first criterion, from two to several dozen actions were reported, and on the second criterion, from none to several dozen detailed descriptions.

Since the use of achievement data to solve achievement problems is a significant aspect of practical leadership at the school level, these findings merit attention. Awareness of these problems is high and relatively uniform among principals. But active behavior, the number of actions, and actions which are specific and clear may differ from principal to principal. Some of those differences may be large indeed, at least as reflected by what the surveyed principals wrote about the problems. The differences may even be larger in actual practice. How principals actually carry out their views on student achievement in this domain of leadership may be most revealing.

Summary

While the California study presumed to constitute an examination of principals' engagement in outcome-based evaluation, it was, in fact, only an examination of principals' views about that engagement. The following conceptual synthesis of the study may be offered, with the overall assumption that the use of achievement data is an integral part of school leadership. First, principals are committed to the theory that their efforts will influence student achievement. Second, they also possess at least some control over how they use data on student achievement. Third, principals do use the data to evaluate achievement. Fourth, that use can be effective. Fifth, principals hold themselves accountable for that use. And sixth, principals do become directly involved with student achievement problems.

Clearly, much more may be learned about outcome-based evaluation as part of school leadership. But it must be more specifically conceptualized, defined, directly observed, recorded, and discussed with principals themselves. Evaluation as part of school leadership obviously involves other topics that have not been explored. It may even be productive to pursue the study of evaluation in school leadership without regard to outcome issues. Part III of this volume presents some preliminary work on this topic.

Part III

Critical Needs as Principals Perceive Them

Part III of this volume focuses on evaluation as a fundamental component in school leadership. In so doing, it departs from evaluation as only an externally mandated activity and from the specific need of principals to respond to the demand that they engage in outcome-based evaluation. It studies instead how principals operate on the basis of critical needs as they themselves perceive them. To be sure, the focus here has been stimulated by the recent developments in and about evaluation in education, but the purpose of this part of the volume is more general. It hopes to provide a preliminary answer to the following question: what is evaluation as a component in school leadership, or what, in the role of principal, can be labeled evaluation?

This part of the volume is based on research recently conducted at the University of California, Santa Barbara. The next four chapters represent a report on a sequence of those studies.

Chapter *13*

Evaluation in Leadership Tasks: Molitor

Awareness of the Concept

Even before the increased visibility and systematization of educational evaluation, evaluators and administrators had been concerned with highly similar issues. They identified problems and recognized the need to solve some of them. They collected information, analyzed it, developed alternative solutions, and examined the consequences of those solutions (e.g., Griffiths 1959; Glasman 1974). The demarcation between evaluation and administration was viewed as largely unclear and perhaps unnecessary. The only difference that seemed clear was that evaluation produced recommendations for decisions, and that administration involved decision making.

In recent years, educational evaluation has been defined in more depth than in the past. This definition is predicated on at least three assumptions: (1) the evaluation component actually exists, (2) it exists along with several other components, and (3) it is not necessarily identical to evaluation in general.

Until the 1970s, evaluation was defined as possessing information and judging the worth of that information. Stufflebeam et al. (1971) suggested that evaluation is a part of leadership in the sense that it creates the information on which leaders make decisions. Glasman and Sell (1972) studied this connection. They defined information as facts and the judgment of its worth as values. All decisions were found to be based on both facts and values, but the specific ratios of one to another varied with each decision. They suggested that when additional and contradictory facts were acquired, decisions based more on values

123

were less likely to be changed than decisions based more on facts. They also suggested that additional facts may be considered significant only if facts were originally considered more significant than values.

Glasman and Bilazewski (1979) studied evaluation as an aspect of school leadership in a different way. Administrators were presented with an extensive summary of a variety of definitions. The summary was based on six major volumes on evaluation in education at the time. The study assumed that the extent to which administrators would view the summary as useful to their work would indicate how much they view evaluation as part of their work. Over half the administrators found the summary "very useful," and most of the rest found it "somewhat useful." The lower the level of the administrator in the administrative hierarchy, the more likely he or she was to view the summary as "somewhat" rather than "very" useful. The study therefore suggested that lower-level administrators are less certain about the function of evaluation in their job than higher-level administrators.

The 1972 and the 1979 studies made specific definitions of evaluation and specific descriptions of how those definitions function in leadership. The studies only assumed a definition of the evaluation component concept and a method of ascertaining that the concept represents reality. On the basis of these assumptions, the findings suggest that evaluation as an activity of school leaders is not an unrealistic concept.

The second assumption is that evaluation is only one of many parts to school leadership. All the other components need to be identified and verified, and again, choices must be made. Some of those other common components are planning, resource acquisition and allocation, personnel guidance, and program development and administration. Evaluation is not viewed as the most prominent duty of the leader, only one of several duties.

The third assumption is that evaluation as a part of another whole and evaluation as a separate whole are not necessarily identical. In other words, evaluation as practiced by school leaders cannot be identical to evaluation as practiced by professional evaluators because it is tied to the leadership role.

We have not come about easily to an awareness that evaluation as a component of school leadership is not necessarily identical to evaluation as a separate entity. Evaluation designs developed by professional evaluators have not been compatible with practical administrative implementations of those designs (McLaughlin 1984). The discrepencies between the designs and the realities in school leadership have been gradually recognized, but their reduction has been slow to emerge.

The Concept from the Principal's Perspective

State law and school district policies specify the evaluation responsibilities of school principals. An investigation of pertinent written materials on the subject was conducted at the University of California, Santa Barbara, in 1980 (Molitor 1981). The investigation revealed that principals' evaluation responsibilities were more clearly specified for secondary than for elementary schools. It also revealed that the job description of secondary school principals was, on the whole, more specifically delineated than that of elementary school principals. This difference was perhaps due to the larger size of secondary schools and to the existence of other administrators, such as deans and assistant principals, in those schools.

Molitor (1981) attempted to identify secondary school principals' opinions about their evaluation responsibilities. A pilot examination revealed that they discuss their evaluation responsibility relatively freely, perhaps because those duties are somewhat distant from all of the day-to-day operations in the school, and also perhaps because of principals' relatively high administrative status (Glasman and Bilazewski 1979).

Molitor decided to seek principals' opinions about their specific administrative tasks. He constructed a list of tasks on the basis of written materials in California, including the California Education Code, the Administrative Code, the Health and Safety Code, and other applicable codes. The materials also included legislation in California which deals with evaluation, local school board regulations about evaluation in two relatively large school districts in southern California, and job descriptions of secondary school principals in these two districts. Molitor pilot-tested the list with ten principals selected at random from each of the two districts. He tested for validity, reliability, and the following two additional criteria:

(1) the extent to which each task was required for the job by district policy and by job description; and

(2) the extent to which all such tasks were included in the list.

The final list of 52 tasks which Molitor used for further examination is presented in table 13.1.

Six principals were chosen at random from the two districts. They were phoned and asked to be interviewed, and all six agreed. Each was ultimately interviewed twice for a total of five to six hours. In the interviews, they were asked two questions with regard to each of the 52 tasks:

(1) What proportion of time do you spend on evaluation in the context of this task?

(2) What do you do when you evaluate?

Molitor defined evaluation at the beginning of each interview as "collecting information and judging its worth for decisions which you make." He asked principals to estimate the proportion of time they devote to evaluation in performing each of the tasks. Weldy (1974) also asked principals to estimate the time spent on certain duties. Other researchers have used other approaches. Jones (1955), McAbee (1958), Lamb (1961), and Triplett (1961) estimated time themselves. Moore (1975) and Wolcott 1973) used still other methods to estimate time. Methods of time measurement vary: one can observe, log, and measure; one can ask principals to do so; one can estimate; and one can ask principals to estimate. The choice depends on the purpose of the study, the tasks involved, and what is already known (Griffiths 1959; Cuttitta 1974; Lipham and Hoeh 1974; Gorton 1976). Molitor did not know what to observe and log, since no prior data existed on evaluation time. He asked for estimates and probed by saying, first, "as much as 100 percent" or "as little as 0 percent", and later, "as much as" (or "as little as") 50 percent, 75 percent (or 25 percent), etc. He recorded the percentages in 12.5 percent increments. Each interview was tape-recorded in its entirety.

Results

The means and standard deviations of principals' estimated evaluation time are displayed in table 13.1. Evaluation time over all 52 tasks was 73 percent. Means of evaluation time by domain ranged from 62.5 percent (school plant) to 81.4 percent (instructional and curriculum development). Evaluation time by tasks varied from 25 percent to 98 percent. Fourteen tasks were reported to constitute at least 90 percent evaluation time: A1, A2, A3, A4, A11, B1, B3, B8, B9, B10, D6, D8, E1, and G5. Five tasks were reported to constitute less than 50 percent evaluation time: A6, B11, C4, E5, and F4.

There may be at least three reasons for the large variation in reported evaluation time by administrative task. One reason may be that evaluation time is a function of task time. Time in Molitor's study was estimated in percentages, not minutes. Had time been measured in minutes and had both task time and evaluation time been measured, it may have been found that the longer the task was, the longer was its evaluation component. Another reason may be that evaluation time is a function of task importance. The more important a task, the longer was its evaluation. Staff recruitment and assignment, for example, may be viewed by principals as highly important and therefore requiring 90.6 percent and 98.1 percent evaluation time, respectively. Attendance in district meetings may be viewed as not too important and therefore requiring only 33.3 percent evaluation time.

There may be a third reason for the large variation in reported evaluation time by task. Evaluation time may be an inverse function of how routine a given task is. Highly routinized tasks such as supervision of cafeteria operation and accounts, for example, require only 25.8 percent evaluation time. Coordination of special programs or formulation of goals and objectives for next year are not routinized and therefore require as much as 94.4 percent and 98.1 percent, respectively. Thus if a task is very routine, it may not require much evaluation.

The principals' answers to the question "What do you do when you evaluate?" were analyzed for their content. Most of their answers — 295 out of a total of 310 (95.1 percent) — focused on information used to make decisions. Five sources of information were detected in their answers:

   (1) their own observations: mentioned in 285 of 295 of the cases (96.6 percent);

   (2) staff input: 119 of the cases (40.1 percent);

   (3) student input: 58 of the cases (19.5 percent);

Table 13.1 Time Principals Spend in Evaluation Activities

Subject	Task	Evaluation percentage	Standard deviation
A Staff personnel	1. Assignment	90.6	9.0
	2. Recruitment	98.1	4.1
	3. Performance evaluation of certificated staff	92.5	9.5
	4. Performance evaluation of classified staff	96.2	8.1
	5. Climate improvement	83.3	13.8
	6. Selection and assignment of substitutes	27.7	13.8
	7. Schedule preparation and modification	77.7	23.0
	8. Supervision assignment of school events	68.4	24.8
	9. Administration of collective bargaining agreements	61.1	29.3
	10. Decisions on tenure, layoffs, and promotions	74.0	29.2
	11. Discipline	96.2	8.1
	Total	78.7	15.7
B Pupil personnel	1. Provision of counseling services	92.5	9.5
	2. Establishment and enforcement of attendance policies	83.5	18.0
	3. Establishment and enforcement of discipline policies	92.5	7.4
	4. Development and coordination of extracurricular programs, including interscholastic sports	72.2	13.8
	5. Establishment of policies on pupil performance reports	68.4	29.7
	6. Coordination with student government	66.6	22.4
	7. Organization of student registration	77.7	26.8
	8. Scheduling pupils	94.4	7.6
	9. Establishment and monitoring of student transfer policies in special classes and other schools	98.1	4.1

Table 13.1 Time Principals Spend in Evaluation Activities (*continued*)

Subject	Task	Evaluation percentage	Standard deviation
	10. Provision for supervision of campus and activities	90.6	8.9
	11. Supervision of student health services	40.6	22.4
	Total	79.7	15.5
C Community-school relations	1. Attendance to parental complaints	81.4	19.2
	2. Work with parent groups	62.8	13.7
	3. Development and coordination of public relations policies	74.0	17.0
	4. Attendance in district meetings	33.3	12.9
	5. Planning and coordination of special events such as graduation, awards	61.1	25.6
	Total	62.5	19.5
D Instruction and curriculum development	1. Development and implementation of courses of study	77.7	28.3
	2. Approval of textbooks, instructional supplies, and equipment	75.8	16.7
	3. Guidance in formulation and revisions of curriculum objectives	70.3	24.9
	4. Coordination of library activities	83.3	13.8
	5. Development and administration of testing programs	62.8	18.8
	6. Provision of teachers' attendance in conventions and conferences	98.1	4.1
	7. Provision of inservice education of certificated staff	88.8	18.2
	8. Coordination of special programs	94.4	7.6
	Total	81.4	16.5
E School finance and	1. School budget preparation	98.1	4.1
	2. Reacquisition approvement	85.1	19.8

Table 13.1 Time Principals Spend in Evaluation Activities (*continued*)

Subject	Task	Evaluation percentage	Standard deviation
business management	3. Supervision of student body finances	66.6	18.2
	4. Office management	87.0	8.9
	5. Supervision of cafeteria operation and accounts	25.8	22.1
	Total	72.5	16.6
F School plant	1. Establishment of a plant maintenance and operation system	57.8	31.8
	2. Development of plan for plant growth and reduction	83.3	19.3
	3. Administration of supplies and equipment	53.6	28.5
	4. Decisions on requests by outside groups to use school facilities	44.4	32.1
	5. Planning vandalism prevention programs	77.7	27.6
	Total	63.3	29.9
G General tasks and planning	1. Organization and conduct of meetings	66.6	15.3
	2. Attendance in conferences and conventions	62.8	22.1
	3. Directing work of administrative assistants	88.8	15.3
	4. Attendance in school functions, such as plays, awards	50.0	21.4
	5. Formulation of goals and objectives for next year	98.1	4.1
	6. Coordination of audio-visual services	82.2	16.1
	7. Master calendar preparation	70.3	18.8
	Total	72.7	16.0
TOTAL		73.3	18.5

Source: Adapted from Molitor (1981).

(4) parent input: 30 of the cases (10.2 percent); and

(5) data from records: 14 of the cases (4.7 percent).

As it turned out, a variety of sources of information was used, but principals relied heavily on personal observations.

Molitor's study reveals that secondary school principals devote a great amount of task time to evaluation and consider evaluation as mainly dealing with information they need for decision making. The heavy reliance on personal observation as a source of information certainly reinforces the notion that evaluation in school leadership is a highly personal activity.

Chapter *14*

Evaluation and Decisions: Gally

Purpose and Method

Molitor's 1981 effort, as summarized in the previous chapter, was a first attempt to give the concept of evaluation, as a component in school leadership, some practical meaning. This preliminary attempt had several shortcomings. The descriptions of the 52 tasks did not include how much time each activity took. Moreover, principals estimated proportion of time rather than absolute time. Molitor did not validate any of the estimates, neither did he seek to examine the substance of the evaluation in a systematic way.

Gally (1982) continued Molitor's preliminary effort. He studied secondary school principals by observing their minute-by-minute activities. He recorded the activities in terms of units, defining a unit as one or more events with a specific content: pedagogical, organizational, supervisorial, etc. Gally implied that there is an instant when the content changes, at which point one unit ceases and another begins. The time which passes between two such instances is the duration of the activity. Pilot studies revealed that the duration of each activity is short — just a few minutes — but that the duration may also vary significantly from unit to unit.

The difficulty in observing the role of evaluation in school leadership is not only that an activity has a short duration. There is also the problem of whether an observation correctly identifies the evaluation component, as well as the problem of how to record that observation. Molitor (1981) provided only the clues that principals believe that much of what they do is evaluation and that evaluation involves handling information for decisions.

133

Gally's study (1982) sought to deal with some of these issues. He chose to observe secondary school principals with the following specific purposes in mind. First, He wanted to test the possibility of reliably detecting the boundaries for each unit of activity. He wanted to measure the duration of each unit by what kind of activity was involved. He reasoned that if the total duration of activities by subject resembled what is known about the kind of activity involved, then he could proceed to further analyze the activities.

Second, Gally wanted to learn more about those activities which end with observed decisions. He wanted to learn about the observability of a decision and the situations which lead to decisions. More specifically, he wanted to know about their duration, where they take place, what the principal does, who participates, who initiates, and in what direction the information is disseminated.

Finally, Gally wanted to learn something about the distribution of units of activities which end with observed decisions; that is, he wanted to classify them by decision evaluation types and corresponding evaluation considerations. For this purpose he used Stufflebeam's (1974a) Context, Input, Process, Product (CIPP) model of types and corresponding decision correlates. This model contained four pairs. The first was labeled "planning decisions," which determine goals and objectives. These decisions are nurtured by "context evaluation" considerations, which involve identifying needs and underlying causes. The second was labeled "structuring decisions," which specify procedures and requirements associated with personnel, facilities, budget, and time. "Input evaluation" considerations nurture these decisions. Evaluation here involves identifying and assessing the relative worth of competing strategies and design. The third was labeled "implementing decisions," which institute procedures, modify schedules, and prepare staffs. These decisions are nurtured by "process evaluation" considerations, which involve assessing the extent to which designs are actually being carried out. The fourth was labeled "recycling decisions," which continue, modify, and terminate activities. They are nurtured by "product evaluation" considerations, which involve describing and judging the outcomes of activities.

Gally's study was conducted in Israel. However, because what is being discussed in this part of the volume is a fundamental phenomenon of school principals' behavior, this fact should not be distracting. Gally's observations took place in September 1981. Eight principals were observed for two weeks, five days per week, and five hours per day. Observers were pretrained to observe and record their observations. The training lasted until the reliability among all 8 observers in a pilot study of 2 principals reached 0.900. The data were grouped by predetermined categories.

Gally chose the 8 principals on the basis of a stratified random sample of all secondary school principals in two of the six counties in Israel. The stratification was based on the size of school in numbers of students, the age of the principal, how many years the principal had been in administration, the principal's formal academic training, and the size of the community in which the school was located. School size among the eight schools ranged from 802 to 2797 students. Age ranged from 43 to 62, and experience ranged from 6 to 30 years. Academic background ranged from B.A. to Ph.D. The size of the community ranged from a small rural town to a large city. Gally justified the size of the sample (only eight principals) on the basis of the study's purposes and on other studies with similar purposes: Burns (1957) used 4 principals; Carlson (1957), 9; Landsberger (1962), 3; Brewer and Tomlinson (1964), 6; Dubin and Sprya (1964), 8; Kelley (1969), 4; Mintzberg (1973), 5; Sproull (1977), 5; and Duignan (1980), 8.

Gally told the principals in advance that their daily activities are of interest to students of educational administration. All eight principals agreed to be observed. Gally chose not to tell them the exact purposes of the study because he believed that this awareness might significantly distort their behavior (see Gulick and Urlick 1937; Carlson 1957; Simon 1975, 1960; Lindblom 1959; Likert 1961; March 1965; Fielder 1966; Weick 1968; Mintzberg 1973; Wolcott 1973; Sproull 1977, 1981).

Results

The total observation time was 24,000 minutes. Activities were observed for a total of 21,608 minutes (90 percent of the time). The mean duration of each activity was 9.5 minutes. Table 14.1 displays the distribution of these activities by number and duration.

Of 2,170 observed activities, 618 (28.5 percent) included observed decisions. Of the 2,102 observed activities in the five major administrative domains (the first five activities in table 14.1), 603 (23.4 per-

Table 14.1 Attributes of Various Administrative Activities

Subject of observed administrative activities	Number of activities	Percentage of all activities	Duration of activities (minutes)	Percentage of total duration	Mean duration of an activity (minutes)
Instruction	631	29.0	6,346	26.4	10.0
Students	434	20.0	3,130	13.0	7.2
Auxiliary services	345	15.9	2,277	9.5	6.6
Public relations	367	17.0	4,320	18.0	11.8
Coordinating functions	325	15.0	3,747	15.6	11.5
Mandatory teaching	33	1.5	1,500	6.3	45.0
Other	35	1.6	288	1.2	8.2
Total	2,170	100.0	21,608	90.0	9.5

Source: Adapted from Gally (1982).

cent) included observed decisions. The following is the distribution of the 603 activities by mean duration of activity:

(1) 11.3 percent lasted up to 1 minute on the average;

(2) 48.2 percent lasted up to 5 minutes on the average;

(3) 68.8 percent lasted up to 10 minutes on the average;

(4) 80.0 percent lasted up to 15 minutes on the average; and

(5) 99.2 percent lasted up to 1 hour on the average.

Thus, 57.5 percent of the 603 activities lasted between 1 and 10 minutes; 31.2 percent, more than 10 minutes; and 11.3 percent, less than 1 minute each.

Other findings include the following:

(1) 90.4 percent of the 603 activities took place in the principals' office;

(2) 9.6 percent took place in the teachers' lounge;

(3) 95.7 percent included speaking to others face to face or on the phone;

(4) 3.3 percent included writing, reading, and/or inspecting;

(5) 33.0 percent included the participation of teachers;

(6) 25.2 percent included the participation of an assistant principal;

(7) 10.3 percent included the participation of other staff;

(8) 34.1 percent included the participation of other individuals;

(9) 25.0 percent were initiated by the principal;

(10) 25.2 percent were initiated by the teachers;

(11) 20.1 percent were initiated by the secretary;

(12) 8.0 percent were initiated by the assistant principal;

(13) 22.1 percent were initiated by other individuals;

(14) 33.7 percent involved the principal receiving information;

(15) 62.0 percent involved the principal and others exchanging information; and

(16) 4.3 percent involved the principal seeking information.

All 603 activities which included observed decisions also involved some evaluation. The distribution of those activities by type as conceptualized by Stufflebeam (1974a), their aggregate mean duration per activity, and the percentage of each which was initiated by the principal are displayed in table 14.2. As can be seen from this table, over one-half of the activities involved structuring decisions, and almost one-third of the activities involved implementing decisions. Activities involving recycling decisions had the longest duration. The largest proportion of activities initiated by the principal also involved recycling decisions.

Table 14.2   Attributes of Activities Ending with Observed Decisions

Type of decision	Number of activities	Percentage of all activities	Mean duration per activity (minutes)	Percentage of activities initiated by the principal
Planning decision (context evaluation)	69	11.3	6.8	17.0
Structuring decision (input evaluation)	306	50.8	8.7	20.0
Implementing decision (process evaluation)	194	32.2	13.9	33.0
Recycling decision (product evaluation)	34	5.7	24.8	43.0
Total	603	100.0		

Source: Adapted from Gally (1982).

Comments

Gally established that boundaries of activities can be observed. The number and duration of those activities correspond closely to what is known about those types of activities in secondary schools in Israel (Gally 1982, Chapter 5). About one-quarter of the observed activities ended with observed decisions. He found that almost 60 percent of those activities lasted between 1 and 10 minutes; over 90 percent were in the principal's office; over 95 percent included speaking to others; over 90 percent included the physical presence of others; about 25 percent were initiated by the principal; over 60 percent involved an exchange of information; and in over 33 percent the principal only received information.

Using Stufflebeam's evaluation-decision typology, Gally found that over 50 percent of the units of activities involved structuring decisions and over 30 percent implementing decisions. Thus, over 80 percent of the decisions deal with procedures rather than goals (planning decisions) or outcomes (recycling decisions). Recycling decisions took the longest per unit of activity. These decisions involve product evaluation, which takes quite a bit of time. Over 40 percent of these units were initiated by the principal, who presumably cares about finding out what the outcomes are.

Gally's findings on the average duration of a unit of activity are significant. It seems that principals handle information on a given content, evaluate it, and sometimes decide within an average span of less than 10 minutes. They experience several of these 10-minute units every day. Most of those units occur in their office and in the presence of other people. At the beginning of each activity, principals mostly react to other peoples' input. As the activity continues, they either exchange or receive information. Gally did not examine what their role is in that exchange.

Gally's findings about decision types are also significant. He found that input and process evaluation goes on in the daily and hourly work of principals. They identify and assess the relative worth of competing strategies and designs, and on that basis consider and sometimes decide immediately by specifying procedures. They also assess the extent to which designs are actually being carried out, and on that basis consider and sometimes decide immediately about instituting procedures, modifying schedules, and preparing staffs. They also seem to make many judgments when they engage in these activities. Gally did not examine the judgmental aspect of those evaluations; he only implied that it exists.

Chapter *15*

Evaluation and Decisions: Lear

Purpose and Method

This study (Lear 1985) sought to observe elementary school principals in California. Like Gally, Lear also wanted to test the possibility of reliably detecting the boundaries of administrative activities and to measure the duration of those activities by type. Like Gally, Lear also wanted to learn where the activities take place, what form of action they take, who participates, and who initiates. Gally examined, in this regard, activities which involve externally observed decisions and found that one-quarter of those activities involved such decisions. Lear sought to examine all activities which were observed, including those which did not involve externally observed decisions. He reasoned that evaluation may involve observed and unobserved decisions and may even involve no decision making.

Lear also extended Gally's inquiry in other ways. He sought to measure the frequency of those activities which involve observed decisions but not observed evaluations, and the distribution of those activities by Stufflebeam's decision types and their mean duration. He also wanted to measure the frequency of those activities which involve observed evaluations but not observed decisions, the distribution of those activities by their evaluation components, and the mean duration of each.

Lear defined evaluation components independently of decision types and in the form of three sets of observed actions. One set involved *information sharing*, which the evaluation literature suggests is one component (Nevo 1983), and which Molitor (1981) mentioned to the principals he interviewed. Gally (1982) observed information sharing without preconceiving it as a part of evaluation. The second set involved the principal's *passing a judgment* on the worth of the information. This component is also suggested in the evaluation literature (Nevo 1983) and is discussed as part of the principal's leadership behavior (Glasman 1979b). Suchman (1967) suggests that it is logical and rational and in no need of objective evidence to support it. Glasman and Sell (1972) suggest that it is rooted in educational idealogies and in the personal values and sentiments of administrators. Gally (1982) suggests that judgment can be observed. The third set of observed actions included *"anything else* which might be observed as part of the evaluation process." Lear's purpose of including this set was to avoid limiting the attention of observers to only what has already been suggested as components of evaluation.

Lear sought to achieve two additional purposes in his study. One was to measure the frequency of those activities which involved both observed decisions and observed evaluation components as defined above, as well as the distribution of these activities by evaluation component, mean duration and decision type. The other purpose was to measure the frequency of more detailed evaluation components and the distribution of these components by decision type. This was to be done within the context of activities which included both observed decisions and observed evaluations.

The rationale for this second purpose was that the more detailed the definition of evaluation components, the more likely one is to learn about the substance of evaluation. Lear used an unpublished study by Glasman (Glasman 1983c) as a point of departure. Glasman observed two elementary school principals in March of 1983. One principal worked in a school in Santa Barbara, California, and the other in a school in Beer sheva, Israel. Glasman observed each principal for five consecutive days from 8:00 a.m. to noon and grouped their activities into nine categories. Three dealt with awareness of information, three others with review of information, and the last three with passing judgement on the worth of the information. The first three involved only information transfer, the second only discussions about information without judgments, and the third only judgments. Each of these three sets included one category of passive behavior on the part of the principal, one category of active behavior which focused on self, and one category of active behavior which focused on delegating a task to others. Glasman recorded 20 hours of activities for each of the two principals and detected at least 10 instances of each of the nine categories. Lear used these categories to define evaluation components in detail.

Lear and three assistants observed 16 principals during January, February, and March of 1984. Each observed one principal for one week. The mean total hours observed per principal was 29.2, and the range was 24.4 to 34.3 hours. The mean daily hours observed per principal was 5.8, and the range was 4.9 to 6.9. Observers were pretrained to observe and record their observations. The training lasted until reliability among all four observers in a pilot study of two principals reached 0.900. Data were recorded by predetermined categories.

Lear chose the 16 principals in the following manner. He contacted 21 principals in four suburban K-6 elementary school districts in the central California coast. The districts were adjacent to each other. Lear requested the principals to participate in the study, and 16 agreed. Of those 16 principals, 12 were males and 4 were females. Their age ranged from 34 to 55 with a mean of 47. Their tenure in education ranged from 10 to 31 years with a mean of 22. Their tenure as principals ranged from 1 to 22 years with a mean of 11. These ranges are not atypical of elementary school principals in California (Wolcott 1973). The number of students enrolled in each of the 16 schools ranged from 310 to 660 with a mean of 438.

Lear told the principals in advance that their daily activities are of interest to students of educational administration. Like Gally, Lear chose not to inform the 16 principals about the exact purposes of the study (see chapter 14).

Results

The total observation time was 28,080 minutes. The number of observed activities was 5,260, averaging 329 per principal and varying between 238 and 419 among the 16 principals. The mean daily number of observed activities per hour for all principals was 11.3 (7.4–16.5).

The largest number of observed activities involved student care and affairs (42 percent). Other activities included

(1) staff and teacher affairs (13 percent);

(2) instruction in the classroom (12 percent);

(3) plant and equipment (10 percent);

(4) PTA and public relations (7 percent);

(5) other (16 percent).

The mean duration of an activity was 5.4 minutes. More detailed data on the duration of activities are as follows:

(1) activities lasting 2 minutes or less, 37 percent;

(2) activities lasting more than 3 minutes but less than 6 minutes, 29 percent;

(3) activities lasting between 6 and 10 minutes, 20 percent; and

(4) activities lasting more than 10 minutes, 14 percent.

The largest number of activities took place in the principal's office (54 percent), involved speaking with others face to face or on the phone (75 percent), involved participation with one or more individuals (77 percent), and were initiated by the principal (63 percent). More detailed data on those distributions are as follows:

(1) location: principal's office, 54 percent, school office, 17 percent; school grounds, 10 percent; classroom 9 percent; and teachers' room, 6 percent;

(2) form: speaking, 75 percent; and reading, writing, or inspecting, 23 percent;

(3) participation: alone, 23 percent; teachers, 22 percent; students, 12 percent; secretary, 11 percent; district office staff, 8 percent; parents, 5 percent; custodian, 3 percent; and teacher's aid, 2 percent; and

(4) initiation: principal, 63 percent; teachers, 13 percent; secretary, 7 percent; students, 4 percent; district office staff, 4 percent; parents, 3 percent; and custodian, 1 percent.

Table 15.1 Duration and Percent Distribution of Observed Activities by Type of Decision and Evaluation Component

Type of activity	Mean duration		Distribution by decision type (percent)				Distribution by evaluation component (percent)			
	Activity	Evaluation component	Planning	Struc-turing	Imple-menting	Recycling	Sharing and judging	Sharing	Judging	Something else
All activities (5,260 activities)	5.4									
Decisions only (1,762 activities, 33% of total)	5.0		29	18	40	13				
Evaluations only (2,114 activities, 41% of total)	7.7	2.7					51	23	6	20
Decisions and evaluations (1,384 activities, 26% of total)	5.7	2.0	28	19	39	14	49	24	8	19

Source: Adapted from Lear (1985).

Table 15.1 summarizes the duration and percent distribution of the 5,260 observed activities by type of decision and evaluation component.

Only Lear himself recorded the nine more detailed categories of evaluation components; the other three observers did not. Of the 1,384 activities with observed decisions and observed evaluation subcomponents, Lear observed 527 (40 percent). In these 527, he detected the following number of each of the nine evaluation components:

(1) 431 instances in which the principal was presented with information (81.8 percent),

(2) 196 instances in which the principal collected information (37.2 percent),

(3) 94 instances in which the principal asked that information be collected (17.8 percent),

(4) 220 instances in which the principal was asked to review information (41.7 percent),

(5) 511 instances in which the principal initiated a review of information (97.0 percent),

(6) 341 instances in which the principal asked for a review of information (64.5 percent),

(7) 99 instances in which the principal was asked to judge the worth of information (18.8 percent),

(8) 473 instances in which the principal judged the worth of information (89.7 percent), and

(9) 161 instances in which the principal asked for a judgment on the worth of information (30.6 percent).

The total number of instances observed and recorded was 2,526.

As this list shows, the principal most frequently initiated a review of information. The next most frequent instances were when a principal initiated judgment on the worth of the information (in almost 5 of 6 cases), and when information was presented to the principal (in over 4 of 5 cases). The next most frequent instance was when a principal initiated a request to review the information (in almost 2 of 3 cases). Each of the rest of the five instances were observed in less than 42 percent of the cases. It seems, then, that the most common pattern leading to a decision is the following: The principal is presented with information; he or she either initiates a review of the information or asks for a review; and he or she passes a judgment on the worth of the information. In all of these cases, a decision was made and externally observed.

When the total of 2,526 instances were cross-tabulated with decision types, 16.9 percent of the instances were associated with planning decisions, 17.7 percent with structuring decisions, 50.9 percent with implementing decisions, and 14.5 percent with recycling decisions (see table 15.2). Particularly deviant cases were with component 3 (in all four decision types) and components 7 and 9 (in structuring and recycling decision types) (see table 15.2).

Comments

Some comparisons between Lear's study and Gally's study should first be made, primarily because, as was suggested earlier, fundamental rather than culture-specific behavioral phenomena are at issue.

Lear found proportionally more activities involving student care and affairs than Gally did (see tables 14.1 and page 144). He also found a shorter mean duration for all activities (see table 14.1 and 15.1). It may be that elementary school principals spend more time than secondary school principals on activities directly associated with students. It may also be that elementary school principals are engaged in activities that do not take as much time. At this point, explanations rooted in efficiency or in cultural differences cannot be offered.

Lear found proportionately fewer activities taking place in the principal's office than Gally did (see pages 137 and 144). He also found fewer activities that involved speaking and more activities that were initiated by principals (see page 137 and 144). He found no activities that involved the participation of assistant principals. It may be that elementary school principals spend more time outside their office than do secondary school principals, and that they spend less time speaking and more time initiating activities. Elementary schools generally have no assistant principals.

Table 15.2 Percent Distribution of Nine Evaluation Components in Four Types of Decisions

Type of decision	Percentage of each evaluation component									Percentage of total
	1	2	3	4	5	6	7	8	9	
Planning	15.3	16.4	31.9	19.5	16.5	16.7	17.2	16.3	19.2	16.9
Structuring	16.5	17.6	33.0	18.2	17.2	19.3	29.2	17.3	30.5	17.7
Implementing	51.7	51.2	28.7	51.4	51.7	51.4	53.1	51.7	44.6	50.9
Recycling	16.5	14.8	6.4	10.9	14.6	12.6	0.5	14.7	5.7	14.5
Total	100.0	100.0	100.0	100.0	100.0	100.0	100.0	100.0	100.0	100.0

Source: Adapted from Lear (1985).

Note: The total number of decisions observed was 527, and the total number of evaluations was 2,526.

Lear found proportionately more activities that involved observed decisions than Gally did. He found considerably more planning decisions and fewer structuring decisions, and somewhat more implementing and recycling decisions. The mean duration of each of the activities involving observed decisions was somewhat lower than the mean duration of all activities. The mean duration of activities involving observed decisions was not as highly differentiated by decision type in Lear's study as in Gally's study. For these figures, see tables 14.2 and 15.1. It may be that elementary school principals make proportionately more planning decisions and fewer structuring decisions than do secondary school principals, and that the duration of their activities is not differentiated significantly by decision type.

Lear found that two thirds of all activities involved evaluation. Of these, 80 percent involved sharing information and/or the principal's judging the worth of the information (table 15.1). The rest involved other evaluation considerations. The mean duration of an activity involving an observed evaluation (7.7 minutes) was almost 1.5 times longer than the mean duration of all activities (5.4 minutes) and slightly more than 1.5 times longer than the mean duration of activities which ended with observed decisions but not evaluations (5.0 minutes; see table 15.1). The mean duration of the evaluation component of an activity was about 35 percent (2.7 minutes) of the total mean duration of the activity (table 15.1).

Lear found about the same proportion of activities which involved both observed decisions and observed evaluation components as Gally found. The mean duration of the activities involving both observed decisions and evaluations (5.7 minutes) was about 0.75 times that of the mean duration of activities involving only observed evaluations (7.7 minutes) and only somewhat longer than those involving only observed decisions (5.0 minutes). The distribution of activities by decision type which involved observed decisions and observed evaluations was highly similar to that of the distribution of activities by decision type which involved observed decisions but not observed evaluations.

As can be seen from table 15.1, only 41 percent of all activities contained any of the four evaluation components. Only 26 percent of all activities contained both a decision and an evaluation, and 33 percent contained a decision but no evaluation. Obviously then, outside observers may observe a decision without observing an evaluation, and vice versa. These two possibilities do not necessarily imply that evaluation does not occur when a decision is made, nor that a decision does not occur when an evaluation is made. They merely suggest that evaluations may be conceptualized not only in association with decisions but also by themselves.

As table 15.1 also shows, each activity involving only an externally observed decision lasted, on the average, somewhat less time — about 0.93 — than all activities. This finding may suggest that activities which require immediate decisions are shorter than those which do not.

Each activity which involved only an externally observed evaluation lasted, on the average, 1.14 times longer than activities which involved both an externally observed decision and an externally observed evaluation (table 15.1). This finding may suggest that evaluation for immediate decision making lengthens the activity but not by more than 14 percent.

The finding that over one-third of the time (41 percent) is devoted to evaluation (as observed externally) either implies that evaluation is more easily observed within the context of some externally observed decision, or that some decisions rest more heavily than others on externally observed evaluations, The mean duration of an activity with an observed evaluation but not an observed decision is significantly longer than the mean for all other activities — 7.7 minutes. But here, too, evaluation is externally observed for over one-third of the time. Observed evaluation, then, constitutes about one-third of the activity time regardless of whether a decision is also observed. This possibility gives rise to the notion that evaluation time may have no association with whether or not an immediate decision is observed.

As table 15.1 also shows, the percent distribution of observed decisions by decision types is almost the same whether or not it involves externally observed evaluation. Moreover, the percent distribution of observed evaluations by evaluation component is almost the same whether or not the evaluation is associated with an externally observed decision. These findings reinforce the notions that observed decision types do not differ in the frequency of their evaluation components, and vice versa.

It was also found that many principals were alerted to a problem by someone else. This passive awareness implies, perhaps, that the principal tries to respond to a problem which is raised by others, even though he or she usually (63 percent) initiates contact with others.

The rest of the decision-making process — and, within it, the evaluation process — was defined as an information review stage and a judgment stage. There were high incidences of principals' initiating reviews of information and judging the worth of the information. The dominant pattern is that principals first become passively aware of information and then begin to review and pass judgment on the information. This dominant pattern occurs with all four decision types: about 50 percent of the time with implementing decisions, and between one-sixth to one-seventh of the time with each of the other three decision types (planning, structuring, and recycling decisions) (see table 15.2).

When evaluation was defined as consisting of nine possible components (table 15.2), 50 percent of the implementing decisions were observed to involve evaluation. When evaluation was defined as consisting of only 4 possible components (table 15.1), 39 percent of the implementing decisions were observed to involve evaluation. In this type of decision, the more evaluation is defined in detail, the more likely it is to be observed and recorded. What and how much evaluation is observed is certainly a function of how it is conceptualized. Since a large portion of the principal's work involves making evaluation for implementing decisions, further study of the evaluation component in this type of decision is warranted.

The same does not hold true for evaluation which is associated with the other three types of decisions. When evaluation was defined as consisting of nine components, 16.9 percent and 17.7 percent, respectively, of the planning and structuring decisions were observed to involve evaluation (see table 15.2). When evaluation was defined as consisting of only four components, more rather than fewer of the planning and structuring decisions were observed to involve evaluation: 28 percent and 19 percent, respectively (see table 15.1). Particularly in planning decisions, the frequency of the four evaluation components (28 percent) is almost 180 percent that of the nine evaluation components (16.9 percent). It may be that observable evaluation considerations occur when decisions are made without much detailed planning. It may also be that detailed considerations are not easily observable, particularly when decisions are made quickly. Is it possible that many detailed evaluation considerations associated with planning and structuring decisions are simply not occurring? Or are they occurring in the minds of the principals and are not externally observable? Or, are the principals themselves not cognizant of them?

Evaluation considerations associated with recycling decisions are also of special interest. When evaluation was defined as consisting of 9 subcomponents, 14.5 percent of the recycling decisions were observed to involve these subcomponents (table 15.2). When evaluation was defined as consisting of 4 subcomponents, 14.0 percent of the recycling decisions were observed to involve these subcomponents (table 15.1). These frequencies are extremely similar, particularly in view of the larger differences associated with the other decision types. It may be that evaluation can be observed to occur in a constant frequency with recycling decisions no matter how many components are used to define it. Is it possible that principals' evaluation behavior can be most accurately predicted with recycling decisions? If evaluation behavior of principals is predictable, then what principals do with their information (such as on student achievement) does not have to remain a mystery. In the previous part of this volume, principals' use of such information was studied in a highly preliminary fashion. More research in this area could produce highly valuable information.

Chapter *16*

The Judgmental Component

This chapter is both a summary of Part III and an attempt to focus on the most problematic ingredient of evaluation in school leadership: judgment. The chapter summarizes a fourth study which surveyed the opinions of educational executives with regard to that ingredient.

A Letter to Former Students

October 1, 1984

Dear . . . . .

I have a problem and I need your help. . . . As you well know, my inquiries over the years about evaluation as an administrative function have been shaped by my strong belief that much of what school leaders do is, in fact, evaluation. I used to apologize for doing research which is rooted in a value stance, but I no longer do. It seems that all grown-ups suffer from the same disease.

Most recently, we have collected some preliminary data on the evaluation component in leadership at the school level. We began by defining evaluation for some secondary school principals as "collecting information and judging its worth for decisions which they make." We asked them to estimate the proportion of time which they spend on evaluation in connection with 52 tasks which they perform as principals. The mean percentage of estimated evaluation time was 73. We also asked them to tell us what they do when they evaluate in the context of each of the 52 tasks. The great majority of their answers focused on the information and on its sources. Personal observations turned out to be the most frequently mentioned information source.

We decided to observe additional secondary school principals. This time, we sought actual decisions which they make. We found that, when their activities were viewed as focusing on a specific content, 25 percent of these activities were externally observed to include decisions. Each activity lasted about 10 minutes on the average. The principals themselves initated about 25 percent of the activities. Information exchange was detected in about 60 percent of them.

We decided to use Daniel Stufflebeam's evaluation-decision typology to guide our observations of this second set of secondary school principals. We observed evaluation considerations which were associated with observed decisions. About one-half the evaluation considerations included the identification and assessment of the relevant worth of a variety of strategies which would determine possible decisions. About one third of the evaluation considerations included an assessment of the extent to which the chosen decisions were actually carried out. The longest-lasting individual decision-related evaluation considerations included descriptions and judgments of decision outcomes.

We then wanted to see what elementary school principals do. We sought to detect evaluation considerations with and without connection to externally observed decisions. Each content-specific evaluation consideration lasted about 5 minutes on the average. The principals initiated about two-thirds of these considerations. We found 26 percent of the activities to involve both evaluation considerations and decisions, 38 percent only decisions (these were made pretty quickly), and 41 percent only evaluation considerations.

We conceptualized evaluation considerations in two ways. The first involved singling out the sharing of information and the principal's passing of a judgment about the worth of the information. The second involved singling out who did what in terms of information sharing, information review, and passing a judgment about the worth of the information.

We used the above conceptualizations to guide our observations of these elementary school principals, but only those activities which included observed evaluation considerations and observed decisions (26 percent of the total). Information sharing and/or principal's passing of a judgment about its worth were observed in 80 percent of the activities. The rest involved other evaluation considerations. We then used the second conceptualization of evaluation considerations to observe 40 percent of the original 26 percent of the activities. The most dominant pattern here was as follows. Information is brought to the attention of the principal. The principal initiates a review of the information by either reviewing it him/herself or by asking someone else to do it. The principal then passes a judgment on the worth of the information. In most cases, a decision was observed toward the end of the pattern described above. This pattern turned out to be dominant regardless of the decision's content or type (Stufflebeam).

The mean duration of evaluation time was about 35 percent of the total time devoted to an activity — 2 minutes — regardless of which conceptualization of evaluation was used. When we compared the frequency of occurrence of the dominant pattern of evaluation for each of the two conceptualizations by decision type, we found the following. The pattern of "others informing – principal reviewing – principal judging" occurred significantly more frequently than the pattern of "sharing of information – principal judging" in implementation decisions. The former pattern also was found to occur significantly less frequently in planning and structuring decisions, and about the same as the latter pattern in recycling decisions.

My current students, when they hear about all of the above, think that we have cracked open this evaluation component somewhat. I would like to believe so, too, but I know that we did it with a definite bias. We found some of this component's fundamental elements, but we obviously invented the terminology to describe them. It seems that if the evaluation component is defined as we defined it, it turns out to be central in the school principal's work space, both quantitatively and qualitatively. It also seems that its "information" component is central regardless of how it is conceptualized. Our problem is with the "judgmental" component. Its centrality has to be a strong function of how it is conceptualized; and here is where I need your help.

Whatever it is, the judgmental component lasts very little time, as observed externally, of course. It is very difficult for us to observe it. Even when we observe what we call "information exchange" or "information review," we suspect that at least part of this component is related to judgment. We also know that the "decisions" which we observe are related to judgment. In short, we find it extremely difficult to sort out empirically the judgmental component of evaluation.

I now believe that some more work must be done on conceptualizing this component. I made some additional attempts to solicit some help from principals, but I am having problems. When I talk to principals about what I observe them do, they give me an after-the-fact analysis which elaborates extensively on information and on decisions but not on judgment. When I talk to principals while I observe them, I am obtrusive, and the on-going process in which they are involved ceases to be a natural one. I decided to ask you for help.

I ask you to suggest to me what you think the substance of this judgmental subcomponent might be. I specifically ask you to offer some generalizations about criteria for judging, the substance and structure of judging, and other possible attributes of judging.

My interest is in the judgmental component of the evaluation component in leadership at the school level. You have now been away from the principalship for a while. I am fully aware of that. But you are still engaged in evaluation, I dare say. I am sure that you meet with school principals in your work, at least occasionally. I hope you can share with me some of your perceptions on this judgmental component. Please do not worry about revealing a bias which has not yet been tested scientifically. If you help me, I shall try to test it myself and report the findings to you.

I thank you sincerely in advance.

Respondents and Responses

This letter was sent to 62 individuals. All had studied at one time or another with the author between 1970 and 1980. All had been exposed to the author's earlier ideas about evaluation and school leadership. All had been interested in the topic to various degrees. All had served as school principals before, during, or after having been exposed to the author's ideas about evaluation. All were still in education but had left the principalship when the letter was written to them. Twenty of them had been secondary school principals, and 42 had been elementary school principals.

Forty-five of the 62 individuals responded in some detail. Eleven responded without giving details, and 6 did not respond by January 1, 1985. Of the 45 respondents, 22 were Americans, 16 Israelis, 2 Canadians, 1 British, 1 Dutch, 1 Japanese, 1 Saudi Arabian, and 1 South African. Thirty-nine were males, and 6 were females. Their age in 1984 ranged from 36 to 58. Twenty-one held doctorates, 18 held M.A. degrees, and 6 held B.A. degrees. Their substantive responses ranged from about 100 to 750 words.

Most of the responses lacked a tight internal organization. They included definitions of the judgmental component of evaluation, its purposes, its forms, where it appears within the decision-making or evaluation process, and what principals need if they are to effectively judge the worth of information. Five responses had a tight internal organization and were structured by subheadings which covered some of the categories mentioned above. In most cases, where more than one suggestion was made about a definition, a purpose or a form of the judgmental component, accompanying suggestions were also made about variations which may exist in specific circumstances related to persons or organizations. In some such cases, additional accompanying suggestions were made to the effect that compromises exist between the variety of definitions, purposes, forms, etc., again, as a function of the variety of circumstances.

Of the 45 responses, 4 were highly pessimistic. They included statements about the inability to "objectify" the topic, let alone to study it in any coherent and scientific way. Two of these responses also mentioned the lack of value — scientifically or practically — in examining the topic because, as one individual put it, "the judgmental subcomponent in evaluation is unknown even to those who practice it," and, as the other individual put it, "I do not believe that there is such a thing altogether."

Analysis

The following is a summary of the content analysis of the 41 responses which offered some conceptual descriptions of the judgmental component of evaluation as practiced by school principals. This summary includes suggestions about what judgment in evaluation is (substance), where it appears within the leadership process (location), what its purpose is (objectives), what structure it has (form), and what personal requirements exist which permit the user to practice it effectively (personal prerequisites). No attempt is made to report how many respondents mentioned each item. The summary is merely a list of all of the separate items which were mentioned.

The substance of the judgmental component of evaluation in school principalship was mentioned in association with problem finding and problem solving. One has to judge whether a problem exists, whether it is in need of solving, whether it can be solved, and whether it is desirable to solve it. Judging was associated with how oneself and others perceive each of these issues.

The location of the judgmental component of evaluation in leadership was mentioned primarily in terms of its limits and their sources. It was mentioned as being located anywhere between the time when information processing begins to be guided by some conscious or subconscious intentions and the time when a rationale begins to emerge for a definite decision or for an action directed toward solving the problem. Exactly when the first point occurs was said to depend on whether the principal-evaluator was able to process information in a neutral fashion — without having a vested interest in it. This ability was argued as having definite human limits. Exactly when the second point occurs was said to depend on how well the principal-evaluator was able to withstand internal and external pressure to develop a rationale for a definite decision or for an action associated with closing the matter.

The purposes, or objectives, of the judgmental component of evaluation was either to help solve problems created by others or to help create problems that would be solved by others and/or by oneself.

The first objective was described primarily as concerned with preserving the status quo. The second objective was described primarily as concerned with initiating change. The principals gave examples of considerations whether either objective would apply, including missions, goals, structures, activities, and outcomes.

The form in which the judgmental component appears within evaluation-based leadership was described primarily in two ways. Evaluation was described as diagnosing, providing support, and managing. It was also described as giving attention, articulating a purpose, and engaging in internal and external public relations. One respondent labeled the former description "passing judgment on microdata" and the latter as "passing judgment on macrodata."

The personal prerequisites needed to engage in effective judging were also described in two ways. In one view, the principal was described as first needing a considerable amount of experience and after that the cognitive ability to construct guidelines on the basis of that experience. In the other view, the principal needed to first have a considerable amount of knowledge before he could make judgments and assess their effects.

In some of the responses, detailed examples were given in association with one or more of the categories or subcategories of the above summary. Some examples concerned curricula. Some dealt with issues associated with teacher assignments and with problems which teachers encountered in the classroom. Others dealt with fiscal matters, with districtwide or citywide problems, and with student affairs. Almost all conceivable tasks and duties which elementary and secondary school principals perform were mentioned as examples in the 41 responses. It was interesting to note that the examples chosen were typical of tasks and duties of the particular country involved.

Clearly, some portions of the above summary should come as no surprise to students of school administration or of educational evaluation. For example, the definition of the substance of the judgmental component of evaluation-based leadership somewhat resembles portions of definitions of school administration as problem solving (e.g., Griffiths 1959). Those forms of the substance that are perceptual regardless of their validity are not drastically different from the view of schools as organizations with distinctive cultures (e.g., Mitchell, Ortiz, and Mitchell 1984) or the view of leadership as the shaping of attitudes (e.g., Peters and Waterman 1982). Some of the objectives of the judgmental component, as well as some of the personal prere-quisites for engaging in it, resemble some suggestions offered by others for effective leadership in education (e.g., Rogers, Talbot, and Cosgrove 1984) or in other fields (e.g., Srivastra 1983). Some of the forms of exercising the judgmental component are similar to some of the leadership attributes which were suggested as existing in educa-tional organizations (e.g., Sergiovanni 1984). And some aspects of all of the above — with the exception, perhaps, of the location of the judgmental components — can be found in a variety of writings on and in educational evaluation.

What is significant about the opinions of the respondents is not that a whole new body of knowledge or parts of it were discovered, but rather that when respondents were asked about a new term, they came back with highly familiar terms. The implication is that despite its largely unchartered attributes, the exercise of judgment is assumed to be a part of evaluation. It should be remembered that the respondents described the process of making judgments as part of the process of evaluation (itself a component in school leadership), rather than as an entity in and of itself. It may be valuable to continue to explore this association.

One exciting dimension that could also be explored relates to the statements about the location of the judgmental component. Respondents suggested both the limits of this component and their sources. Limits reflect something about the territory — where it can be found. Sources of limits reflect something about the resiliency and adjustability of the limits. To repeat, the territory which has to be charted lies between the moment school leaders begin to process information and the moment they begin to develop a rationale for a potential decision or action. The timing of the first point can probably be adjusted if leaders are able to control when they begin to inten-tionally process information. The timing of the second point can prob-ably be adjusted if leaders are able to control the effect of external pressure to develop a rationale for their decisions or actions. The more they are able to stretch the territory between these two points, the better their judgment may be. Or could it be that effective leaders combine these two points into one?

Part IV

Conclusion

Chapter 17

Integrating the Facts

This book has presented school leadership as rooted in evaluation. It began by assuming that school leadership is an ability and that evaluation is a natural mental process. It then described demands for evaluation as coming from two sources: the larger society, which has recently intensified its demands for quality in education, and the individual principal, who has always engaged in some evaluation. Sometimes school leaders respond to these demands out of loyalty to the society and its educational institutions, and sometimes they pursue their own volitions on the basis of critical needs as they themselves perceive them.

Three research objectives were set. One was to examine the educational evaluation literature as it pertains to school leaders. Another was to examine how principals engage in evaluation on the basis of student achievement data. And a third was to interview and observe elementary and secondary school principals and describe their engagement in evaluation in association with their other duties.

Living with Demands for Accountability

The need to accomodate directives from society and to also maintain sufficient discretionary powers to continue to lead schools as they see fit forces school principals to give some renewed thought to their role as facilitators of student achievement.

Principals have been found to have a strong orientation toward improving student achievement. They believe it is possible to reduce student learning to specific instructional objectives, to teaching to these objectives so as to improve achievement, to influence teachers to do so, and to use student achievement data to plan their instructional objectives.

Principals also seem to think they have a great deal of control over how they use student achievement data. They report success in formalizing and specifying student achievement data-based instructional objectives, in making these objectives clear to teachers, in measuring student achievement as a function of these objectives, and in extensively sharing student achievement data with their teachers. They also report that they use the data extensively in evaluating educational programs and in reporting on their evaluations to their district office. In all of the above, principals essentially follow district directives. Variation regarding these attitudes and activities is negligible.

However, variation among principals in other pertinent attitudes and activities is high. They vary in how they actually use student achievement data in evaluating teachers, and in their attitudes about the effectiveness and accountability of teachers and of themselves. The large variations here imply a wide variety of opinions as to what is possible and what is not possible, as well as to how much principals actually use their own discretionary power.

Principals are also found to vary widely in the strategies they develop to handle academic problems of low achievers. Here, the mandate issued by school districts is not very specific. Different principals interpret it differently in thought and deed.

Thus, as the pressure from outside agencies as well as from school districts has increased the systematic use of evaluation based on performance results, school principals have followed the directives but have also used their discretionary powers when they wanted and were able to. Even if such pressures lessen, the private evaluation world of school principals cannot easily avoid giving serious attention to student achievement and to schools' efforts to improve student performance.

Living with Daily Evaluation

A realistic concept of evaluation as a part of daily decision making must take into account the many ambiguities associated with decision making in general as well as with school principals' decision making. General administrative decision making lacks complete clarity because of the multiplicity of administrative functions and because of the many acts involved in making a decision and putting it into operation.

For a variety of reasons, school administrative decision making has even less clarity. School goals are highly ambiguous. Although schools are supposed to help a child attain normal adult status, what is normalcy? The limits of school authority are ambiguous. Schools have the right to influence but are strictly limited to what the state demands. The framework within which educational services are delivered is also ambiguous, since schools serve specific purposes as well the general welfare. The definition of learning in schools is likewise unclear. Which permanent, long-term changes in the student's knowledge and skills can be directly attributed to the student's experience in the school environment? And finally, the administrative decision-making process itself is ambiguous. How much, for example, are teachers involved in that process?

To study school leadership and its decision-making dimensions with the aid of evaluation concepts is valuable from at least three perspectives. First, the reasons for a conscious engagement in evaluation seem to be clearer than those for conscious engagement in decision making. Second, conscious evaluation results from conscious recognition of a problem more than does conscious decision making. Moreover, evaluation methods in schools are usually clearer than corresponding decision-making methods. Finally, the expected results of evaluation are easier to describe than those emanating from decision making. While evaluation findings include recommendations for decisions — a presentation of relatively clear choices — decisions are followed by implementations — the many, tedious ways of putting the decision into operation.

When secondary school principals were interviewed about their awareness of information needed for evaluation, they estimated that evaluation took almost three-quarters of their total time. Between-task variations in evaluation time were large and significant. It appears that the less routinize a task, the larger the principals' estimate of the evaluation time needed for the task. The principal spends most of this time assimilating information gained from his or her own observations.

When secondary school principals were observed in action, decisions were detected in one-quarter of their activities, and evaluation considerations were detected in association with preconceived types of decisions, such as planning, structuring, implementing, and recycling decisions. Exchange of information appeared to consume about two-thirds of an activity regardless of the type of decision. While not all activities overtly involved a decision, the connections between exchanging information and rendering a judgment were clear.

The connections between information and judgments were more clearly observed when observations were based on preconceived information-processing and judgment-rendering typologies instead of preconceived decision types. Elementary school principals were observed to render judgment in 1 out of 12 activities, and to simply render judgment in association with information processing in 1 out of 2 activities. In 9 out of 10 activities, the dominant pattern seems to include a review of pertinent information and then a rendering of judgment. In most of these cases, the original information was brought to the attention of the principal by someone else.

The activity of rendering a judgment seems to be the most intriguing of all evaluation components. These judgments probably rely on evidence and arguments which permit school administrators to decide and act. The judgmental component of evaluation, according to experienced educational administrators, is associated with the rise and termination of intentionality. Judgment rendering begins when principals first process information on the basis of some definite intention on their part, and ends when principals first develop a rationale for a definite decision. This endpoint seems to reflect a desire to close matters so as to have a guide for action. The principal's intentionality not only makes rendering judgment a subjective endeavor, but is probably also a mark of flexible thinking and flexible behavior.

This flexibility is a key to understanding school leadership, regardless of which theoretical approach (e.g., Bolman and Deal 1984) is used to study school leadership. If, for example, school goals, roles, and technology are the dominating concepts, then school leaders' flexibility, as exemplified by how they render judgments, can be used to describe how they distribute rewards and penalties to control the activities of their organization. When school leadership is examined, instead, as an interplay between people and the school as an organization, then flexibility, judgment, evaluation, and leadership are described as helping the individual grow and improve so as to better fit the organization. In a third context, power, conflicts, and the distribution of scarce resources are the themes of analysis. Here, leadership, its evaluation component, and its judgment-rendering subcomponent are seen as the exercise of power in managing conflicts. And finally, when the organizational meaning is at stake, then leadership relates to organizational images. Evaluation, judgment rendering, and flexibility all play a role in the shared ritual.

The value of focusing on flexibility in judgment rendering should not be mysterious. After all, flexibililty is required whenever there is uncertainty. What may be new to students of school leadership is that the work which Bruner and Simon began continues until this day, and its focus in cognitive psychology is on judgment research (e.g., Kahneman, Slovic, and Tversky 1982). Bruner worked on strategies of thinking. Simon worked on reasoning and bounded rationality. Both tried to simplify the act of making a judgment. Current cognitive psychologists who work on judgment rather than on choice are sending the message that judgment under uncertainty is central. It is high time that students of school administration admit it too, and set out to examine it rather than be ashamed of it.

Chapter *18*

Further Study

The Focus on Judgment

The subjective element in evaluation-based school leadership has become increasingly apparent toward the end of this volume. This is not a coincidence. The volume began with assumptions about evaluation as a natural mental process. The rendering of subjective judgments is not only inevitable in this process; it is basic to it. That evaluation-based school leadership is being portrayed toward the end of this book in the very specific sense of rendering judgment requires no apology. Any in-depth study requires a specific focus.

Over the last two years or so, I have posed the following question to numerous school administrators: "What do you do other than evaluate constantly and other than render judgments as you evaluate?" The most common answer I received was "I decide" and/or "I act." Often I received the following answer as well: "If that is the way you define evaluation in leadership, then I do nothing else."

Both answers have merit. The first answer implies that to study evaluation in school leadership is to study almost everything that precedes leaders' decisions and actions. The second answer implies that decisions and actions may themselves be objects which are evaluated and about which judgments are rendered. Either way, there is still much uncertainty about leaders' use of evaluation.

It is obviously difficult to study leadership and evaluation in the abstract. If this study is pursued, it will probably have to include decisions and actions, which are more observable than evaluations. Decisions and actions may be viewed as pauses in the ongoing process of mental evaluation. As such, they may reduce some uncertainty about evaluation, just as in physics the notion of particles helped reduce some uncertainty about waves. At the very least, however, they may serve as real or imaginary points in an ongoing natural evaluation process with which behaviors may be associated. If these behaviors are found to have common threads, then they may even add up to a complete picture of evaluation.

Evaluation Behavior

Evaluation behaviors are currently being studied at the University of California, Santa Barbara. These studies are approaching the problem empirically rather than from known and tested theories. In one set of studies, for example, the decision point which was chosen was the announcement by the school principal about which teachers are assigned to which classrooms for the upcoming school year. This example was chosen because teacher assignment is considered by many to be a central and significant activity of principals (e.g., Hansen 1979; Bidwell and Kasarda 1980).

These studies are investigating the behaviors that precede and follow teacher assignments. They focus on how principals use evaluation before they make assignment decisions, and then on how they communicate their evaluations to those who are unhappy with their decisions. The first set of evaluations is described as either "substantive" (dealing with the "core of the matter") or "political" (dealing with "other" people). A substantive evaluation, for example, considers the specific collective educational needs of students in a given classroom or a given teacher's prior performance. A political consideration considers pressure exerted by parents or by the district office. The second set of evaluations is divided in a similar way. The ratio of substantive to political evaluations is then determined in both the pre- and postdecision situations for a sample of principals and for all their assignment decisions in a given year. Preliminary data indicate some measure of consistency between pre-and postdecision evaluations for a given principal over several assignment decisions.

Data are also being gathered on how principals communicate their evaluations to those who are unhappy with some assignment decisions. Preliminary results here indicate that principals tend to spend a long time explaining their substantive considerations when they want to persuade an unhappy person that their decision was reasonable. Other data indicate that they tend to rely on political considerations when they are being apologetic and are taking as little time as possible to convey their apologies to an unhappy person. No theory has yet been developed from these preliminary findings.

Principals' Orientation toward Evaluation

Other current studies at the University of California, Santa Barbara, focus on evaluation orientations of school principals, not necessarily in connection with decision making (e.g., Brown, Newman, and Rivers 1984) and its psychological bases (Vroom and Yetton 1973; Vroom and Yago 1974; Vroom 1976 ; Janis and Mann 1977) nor in connection with demands for evaluation (e.g. Kean 1983; Burry 1984). These new studies are guided by the theories of people's sense of their own effectiveness mainly as a perception about self-control in given situations (e.g., Deci 1975; de Charmes 1976; Harter 1978) and as a perception of how personal efforts shape desired outcomes (e.g., Rotter 1975; Seligman 1975; Bandura 1977; Weiner 1980; Stipek and Weiss 1981; Fuller, Wood, Rapoport, and Dornbusch 1982; Langer 1983; Taylor and Betz 1983). Here, a theory of the role of evaluation in school principals' sense of their effectiveness is being developed. The theory is being tested by studying perceptions, actions, and conceptions relating to evaluation (Duckworth 1979a; Glasman 1984a, 1984b). High scores in these abilities are postulated as reflecting a strong sense of personal effectiveness. Low scores are postulated as reflecting a low sense of effectiveness.

More studies are being contemplated, despite some frustrating experiences — particularly those associated with inevitable methodological compromises. Subjects do not always cooperate, the researcher often obtrudes, and pure laboratory experiments are difficult to conduct. Surveys of subjects who respond orally or in writing have validity problems. Structured observations reveal too little, and open-ended, naturalistic investigations are too time consuming. Finally, amateurish psychoanalysis is more art than science. Not all who practice it are psychologically well put together themselves.

Concluding Remarks

The study of evaluation behavior and orientation in school leadership is nonetheless fascinating. It was prompted by the move to intensify the systematization of evaluation in education. Perhaps this study is not a search for a science of evaluation-based school leadership but rather the pursuit of one more way to describe, interpret, and predict excellence in school leadership.

The view of evaluation-based leadership which this volume has provided is formative in nature. It constitutes an attempt to stimulate further discussion and study of school leadership as based on evaluation. If this view does not ultimately integrate all relevant considerations, there are at least two reasons. One is that, at the present time, the conceptual framework of evaluation-based leadership is only in its initial stages of development. The notion of school leadership as based on evaluation is a new way of viewing leadership. If this view is pursued further and in depth, then a conceptual framework may materialize. Even if a pioneering theory could be developed, its value should be ultimately judged on how long it holds together. The other reason for suspecting that a complete picture is not yet in sight is the painfully long — and at times, endless — distance between behavioral theories and practices. Responsible research does not try to prematurely bridge this gap. The view presented in this volume includes no suggestions or recommendations to administrators regarding their use of evaluation. It ends, rather, with suggestions for a further study of evaluation behavior and orientation of school leaders. Only with additional descriptive work can new interpretations be offered. And only well-researched interpretations have the potential of generating theories which might eventually help guide practice in a useful way.

Bibliography

Adams, J.D. (ed.) 1984, *Transforming Work*, Alexandria, Va.: Miles River.

Alkin, M.C., 1969, "Evaluation Theory Development," *Evaluation Comment*, Vol. 2, No. 2, pp. 2–7.

Alkin, M.C., Daillak, R., and White, P., 1979, *Using Evaluations: Does Evaluation Make a Difference?* Beverly Hills: Sage.

Alkin, M.C., and Glasman, N.S., 1975, "Institutionalizing Accountability," *Policy Planning and Administration in Education*, Vol. 5, No. 1, pp. 48–56.

Alkin, M.C., and Klein, S.P., 1972, "Accountability Defined: Evaluating Teachers for Outcome Accountability," ERIC ED 068 495.

Argyris, C., 1983, "Productive and Counter Productive Reasoning Processes," in Scivasta, S. (ed), *The Executive Mind*, San Francisco: Jossey-Bass, pp. 25–27.

Baker, E.L., and Quellmalz, E.S., 1980, *Educational Testing and Evaluation*, Beverly Hills: Sage.

Bandura, A., 1977, "Self Efficacy: Toward a Unifying Theory of Behavioral Change," *Psychological Review*, Vol. 84, pp. 191–215.

Bank, A., and Williams, R.C., 1985, "Data for Educational Decision Makers: From Program Evaluation to Information Systems," *Studies in Educational Evaluation*, Vol. 11, No. 2, pp. 159–182.

Bank, A., Williams, R.C., and Burry, J. (eds.), 1981, *Evaluation in School Districts: Organizational Perspectives*, Los Angeles: Center for the Study of Evaluation, University of California, Los Angeles.

Barnard, C., 1938, *The Functions of the Executive*, Cambridge: Harvard University Press.

Ben-Dror, G., 1979, *Initial Administrative Steps for Implementing the Reform in the Israeli Educational System: 1968–1972*, unpublished Ph.D. dissertation, University of California, Santa Barbara.

Berk, R.A. (ed.) 1981, *Educational Evaluation Methodology: The State of the Art*, Baltimore: The John Hopkins University Press.

Berk, R.A., and Rossi, P.H., 1977, "Doing Good or Worse: Evaluation Research Politically Reexamined," in Guttentag, M. (ed.), *Evaluation Studies*, Vol. 2, Beverly Hills: Sage.

Berman, P., and McLaughlin, M.W., 1979, *Federal Programs Supporting Educational Change, Vol. 7: Factors Affecting Implementation and Continuation*, Santa Monica, Calif.: The Rand Corporation.

Bickel, W.E., and Cooley, W. W., 1985, "Decision-Oriented Educational Research in School Districts: The Role of Dissemination Processes," *Studies in Educational Evaluation*, Vol. 11, No. 2, pp. 183–204.

Bidwell, C.E., 1965, "The School as a Formal Organization," in March, J.G. (ed), *Handbook of Organizations*, Chicago: Rand McNally.

————, 1973, "The Social Psychology of Teaching," in Travers, R.M.W. (ed.), *Second Handbook of Research on Teaching*, Chicago: Rand McNally.

————, 1977, "The Schools as Formal Organizations: Some New Thoughts," in Getzels, J.W. (ed.), *Problem Finding in Educational Administration*, Chicago: Rand McNally.

Bidwell, C.E., and Kasarda, J., 1975, "School District Organization and Student Achievement," *American Sociological Review*, Vol. 40, No. 2, pp. 55–70.

————, 1980, "Conceptualizing and Measuring the Effects of Schooling," *American Journal of Education*, Vol. 88, pp. 1–30.

Biniaminov, I., 1981, *School Organizational Factors and School Outcomes in the Israeli Secondary Education*, unpublished Ph.D. dissertation, University of California, Santa Barbara.

Bloom, B.S., et al., 1971, *Handbook on Formative and Summative Evaluation of Student Learning*, New York: McGraw-Hill.

Bolman, L.G., and Deal, T.E., 1984, *Modern Approaches to Understanding and Managing Organizations*, San Francisco: Jossey-Bass.

Bossart, S., et al., 1982, "The Instructional Management Role of the Principal," *Educational Administration Quarterly*, Vol. 18, No. 3, pp. 34–64.

Brewer, E., and Tomlinson, J.W., 1964, "The Manager's Working Day," *The Journal of Industrial Economics*, Vol. 12, pp. 191–197.

Brickell, H.M., 1976, "The Influence of External Political Factors on the Role and Methodology of Evaluation," *Evaluation Comment*, Vol. 5, pp. 1–6.

Bridge, R.G., Judd, C.M., and Moock, P.R., 1979, *The Determinants of Educational Outcomes*, Cambridge, Mass.: Ballinger.

Bridges, E.M., 1977, "The Nature of Leadership," in Cunningham, L.L., Hack, W.G., and Nystrand, R.O. (eds.), *Educational Administration: The Developing Decades*, Berkeley: McCutchan, Chapter 10.

Brookover, W.B., et al., 1978, *School Social Systems and Student Achievement: Schools Can Make a Difference*, New York: Praeger.

Brown, R.D., Newman, D.L., and Rivers, L.S., 1984, "A Decisionmaking Context Model for Enhancing Evaluation Utilization," *Educational Evaluation and Policy Analysis*, Vol. 6, No. 4, pp. 393–400.

Burns, T., 1957, "Management in Action," *Operational Research Quarterly*, Vol. 8, pp. 45–60.

Burry, J., (ed.), 1984, *Evaluation Comment*, Vol. 7, No. 1.

Burry, J., Alkin, M.C., and Ruskus, J., 1985, "Organizing Evaluations for Use as a Management Tool," *Studies in Educational Evaluation*, Vol. 11, No. 2, pp. 131–158.

Calfee, R., and Brown, R., 1979, "Grouping Students for Instruction," in Duke, D.L. (ed.), *Classroom Management: The 78th Yearbook for The National Society for the Study of Education*, Part II, Chicago: The University of Chicago Press.

California State Department of Education, 1977, *School Effectiveness Study*, Sacramento, Calif.

Callahan, R.E., 1962, *Education and the Cult of Efficiency*, Chicago: University of Chicago Press.

Campbell, R.F., Corbally, J.E., Jr., and Ramseyer, J.A., 1961, *Introduction to Educational Administration*, Boston: Allyn and Bacon.

Campbell, R.F., Cunningham, L.L., Usdan, M.D., and Nystrand, R.O., 1980, *The Organization and Control of American Schools*, Columbus, Ohio: C.E. Merrill.

Carlson, S., 1957, *Executive Behavior: A Study of the Work Load and the Working Methods of Managing Directors*, Stockholm, Sweden: Stromberg.

Centra, J.A., and Potter, D.A., 1980, "School and Teacher Effects: An Inter-relational Model," *Review of Educational Research*, Vol. 50, No. 2, pp. 273–291.

Coats, W.D., 1975, "Accountability in Education: The Kalamazoo Plan," ERIC ED 106 946.

Cohen, D.K., and Weiss, J.A., 1977, "Social Science and Social Policy: Schools and Race," in Weiss, C.H. (ed.), *Using Social Research in Public Policy Making*, New York: D.C. Heath, pp. 66–83.

Cohen, M., 1981, "Effective Schools: What the Research Says," *Today's Education*, April/May.

Cohen, M.D., March, J.G., and Olsen, J.P., 1972, "A Garbage Can Model of Organizational Choice," *Administrative Science Quarterly*, Vol. 17, pp. 1–25.

Cohn, E., and Millman, S.D., 1975, *Input-Output Analysis in Public Education*. Cambridge, Mass.: Ballinger.

Coleman, J.S., et al., 1966, *Equality of Educational Opportunity*, Washington, D.C.: Government Printing Office.

Cooley, J.G., 1980, *The Role of Personal Controllability in Teacher Receptivity to Evaluation: An Exploratory Study*, unpublished Ph.D. dissertation, University of California, Santa Barbara.

Cronbach, L.J., 1963, "Course Improvement Through Evaluation," *Teachers College Record*, Vol. 64 (May), p. 672.

Cronbach, L.J., et al., 1980, *Toward Reform of Program Evaluation*, Los Angeles: Center for the Study of Evaluation, University of California, Los Angeles.

Cuban, L., 1984, "Transforming the Frog into a Prince: Effective Schools Research, Policy and Practice at the District Level," *Harvard Educational Review*, Vol. 54, No. 2 (May), pp. 129–151.

Cubberly, E.P., 1916, *Public School Administration*, Boston: Houghton Mifflin.

Cunningham, L.L., and Gephart, W.J., 1973, *Leadership: The Science and the Art Today*, Itasca, Ill.: F.E. Peacock.

Cunningham, L.L., Hack, W.G., and Nystrand, R.O. (eds.), 1977, *Educational Administration: The Developing Decades*, Berkeley: McCutchan.

Cuttitta, F.F., 1974, *Decision Making Administrative Behavior: Field Centered Profile of the Urban School Principal*, New York: City University of New York, #10080.

Daillak, R.H., 1980, *Evaluators at Work: A Field Study*, Los Angeles: Center for the Study of Evaluation, University of California, Los Angeles.

Deal, T., and Kennedy, A., 1982, *Corporate Cultures*, Reading, Mass.: Addison-Wesley.

de Charmes, R., 1976, *Enhancing Motivation: Change in the Classroom*, New York: Irvington.

Deci, E., 1975, *Intrinsic and Extrinsic Motivation*, New York: Plenum.

Dilman, D.A., 1978, *Mail and Telephone Surveys*, New York: John Wiley and Sons.

Dornbusch, S.M., and Scott, W.R., 1975, *Evaluation and the Exercise of Authority*, San Francisco: Jossey-Bass.

Dornhoff, G.W. (ed.), 1980, *Power Structure Research*, Beverly Hills: Sage.

Dorr-Bremme, D., 1983, "Linking Testing with Instructional Decision Making," in Bank, A., and Williams, R.C. (eds.), *Evaluation Systems Project*, Los Angeles: Center for the Study of Evaluation, University of California, Los Angeles, pp. 111–154.

Dubin and Sprya, S.L., 1964, "Executive Behavior and Interaction," *Industrial Relations*, Vol. 3, pp. 99–108.

Duckworth, K., 1979a, "Either We're Too Early and They Can't Learn It or We're Too Late and They Know It Already," *Harvard Educational Review*, Vol. 49, No. 3, pp. 297–312.

Duckworth, K., 1979b, "Linking Educational Policy and Management with Student Achievement," ERIC ED 170 394.

Duignan, P., 1980, "Administrative Behavior of School Superintendents: A Descriptive Study," *The Journal of Educational Administration*, Vol. 23, No. 1, pp. 5–26.

Duke, D.L., 1979, "Environmental Influences on Classroom Management," in *Seventy-eighth Yearbook of the National Society for the Study of Education*, Chicago: The University of Chicago Press, pp. 333–362.

———, 1982, "Leadership Functions and Instructional Effectiveness," *NASSP Bulletin* (October), pp. 1–12.

————, 1984, "The Aesthetics of Leadership," unpublished paper, Eugene, Oreg.: Lewis and Clark College.

Duke, D.L., and Imber, M., 1983, *Should Principals Be Required to be Effective? Unpublished paper*, Eugene, Oreg.: Lewis and Clark College.

Easton, D., 1965, *A Systems Analysis of Political Life*, Chicago: The University of Chicago Press.

Ebel, R.L., 1979, *Essentials of Educational Measurement*, Englewood Cliffs, N.J.: Prentice-Hall.

Edmonds, R.R., 1981, "Making Public Schools Effective," *Social Policy*, Vol. 12, No. 2, pp. 56–59.

Eisner, E.W., 1975, "The Perceptive Eye: Toward the Reformation of Educational Evaluation," Stanford, Calif.: *Stanford Evaluation Consortium*.

————, *1979, The Educational Imagination*, New York: Macmillan.

Ellis, A.B., 1975, *Success and Failure: A Summary of Findings and Recommendations for Improving Elementary Reading in Massachusetts City Schools*, Boston: Massachusetts Advisory Council on Education.

Fielder, F.E., 1966, "The Contingency Model: A Theory of Leadership Effectiveness," in Prohansky, H., and Seidenberg, B. (eds.), *Basic Studies in Social Psychology*, New York: Holt, Rinehart and Winston, pp. 538–551.

Firestone, W.A., and Wilson, B.L., 1983, "Using Bureaucratic Linkages to Improve Instruction: The High School Principal's Contribution," Eugene, Oreg.: Center for the Study of Educational Policy and Management, University of Oregon.

Flanders, N.A., and Simon, A., 1969, "Teacher Effectiveness," in Ebel, R.L. (ed.), *Encyclopedia of Educational Research*, New York: Macmillan.

Fredericksen, J.R., and Edmonds, R.R., 1979, *Identification of Instructionally Effective and Ineffective Schools*, Paper presented at the annual meeting of the American Educational Research Association, San Francisco, California, April.

Fuller, B., Wood, K., Rapoport, T., and Dornbusch, S.M., 1982, "The Organizational Context of Individual Efficacy," *Review of Educational Research*, Vol. 52, No. 1, pp. 7–30.

Gally, J., 1982, *The Evaluation Component: An Exploratory Study in Educational Administration*, unpublished Ph.D. dissertation, University of California, Santa Barbara.

Garms, W.I., Guthrie, J.W., and Pierce, L.C., 1978, *School Finance*, Englewood Cliffs, N.J.: Prentice-Hall.

Glaser, R., and Klaus, D.J., 1962, "Proficiency Measurement: Assessing Human Performance," in Gagne, R.M. (ed.), *Psychological Principles in Systems Development*, New York: Holt, Rinehart and Winston.

Glasman, N.S., 1974, "Personnel Evaluation Research: Implications for Instructional Improvement," *The Canadian Administrator*, Vol. 13, No. 6, pp. 29–34.

_____, 1977, "A Proposed Structure for Evaluating Personnel for Decision Making," *Studies in Educational Evaluation*, Vol. 3, No. 1, pp. 47–56.

_____, 1979a, "The Effects of Governmental Evaluation Mandates," *Administrator's Notebook*, Vol. 27, No. 2, pp. 1–4.

_____, 1979b, "A Perspective of Evaluation as an Administrative Function in Education," *Educational Evaluation and Policy Analysis*, Vol. 1, No. 5, pp. 39–44.

_____, 1981, "School Principals and Achievement Tests," unpublished paper, 1981, 96 pp.

_____, 1982, "State Perceptions on State-Wide Evaluation in California," *Politics of Education Bulletin*, Vol. 11, No. 1, pp. 4–7.

_____, 1983a, "Increased Centrality of Evaluation and the School Principal," *Administrator's Notebook*, Vol. 30, No. 7, pp.1–4.

_____, 1983b, "Government Control of School Administration in the United States," *The Journal of Educational Administration and History*, Vol. 15, No. 2, pp. 42–48.

_____, 1983c, "Israel: Political Roots and Effects of Two Educational Decisions," in Thomas, R.M. (ed.), *Politics and Education*, New York: Pergamon, Chapter 9.

_____, 1983d, "Preliminary Data on Districts' Reporting Activities With Regard to Mandated Evaluation," unpublished paper, 45 pp.

_____, 1983e, "Information and the School Principal: How to Find Out What is Going On." unpublished paper, 48pp.

_____, 1984a, The School Principal as Evaluator," *The Administrator's Notebook*, Vol. 31, No. 3, pp. 1–4.

_____, 1984b, "Student Achievement and the Principal," *Educational Evaluation and Policy Analysis*, Vol. 6, No. 3, pp. 55–68.

————, 1984c, "Three Case Studies of Systematized Evaluation in a High School," unpublished paper, 1984, 47 pp.

————, 1986, "Outcome-Based Evaluation of Teachers: Perspectives of Principals," *International Educational Administration* (in press).

Glasman, N.S., and Bilazewski, B.V., 1979, "The Practicing Administrator-Evaluator and Educational Evaluation Literature," *Journal of Educational Administration and History*, Vol. 11, No. 1, pp. 21–33.

Glasman, N.S., and Biniaminov, I., 1981, "Input-Output Analysis of Schools," *Review of Educational Research*, Vol. 51, No. 4, pp. 509–539.

Glasman, N.S., and Paulin, P.J., 1982, "Possible Determinants of Teacher Receptivity to Evaluation," *Journal of Educational Administration*, Vol. 20 (Summer), No. 2, pp. 148–171.

Glasman, N.S., and Sell, R., 1972, "Values and Facts in Educational Administrative Decisions," *Journal of Educational Administration*, Vol. 10, No. 2, pp. 142–163.

Glass, G.V., 1969, *The Growth of Evaluation Methodology*, Boulder, Colo.: Laboratory of Educational Research, University of Colorado, Research Paper #27.

————, 1974, "Teacher Effectiveness," in Walberg, H.J. (ed.) *Evaluating Educational Performance*, Berkeley: McCutchan.

————, 1977, *Standards and Criteria*, Kalamazoo, Mich.: Occasional Paper Series in Evaluation, #10, Evaluation Center, Western Michigan University.

————, 1979, "Policy for the Unpredictable," *Educational Researcher*, Vol. 8 (October), pp. 12–14.

Goldhammer, R., Andersen, R.H., and Krajewski, R.J., 1980, *Clinical Supervision: Special Methods for the Supervision of Teachers*, New York: Holt, Rinehart and Winston.

Gorton, R.A., 1976, *School Administration: Challenge and Opportunity for Leadership*, Dubuque, Iowa: William C. Brown.

Granger, R.L., 1971, *Educational Leadership*, Scanton, Pa.: Intext.

Griffiths, D.E., 1959, *Administrative Theory*, New York: Appleton-Century-Crofts.

_____, 1979, "Another Look at Research on the Behavior of Administrators," in Immegart, G.L., and Boyd, W.L. (eds.), *Problem-Finding in Educational Administration*, Lexington, Mass.: Lexington Books.

Grunsky, O., 1981, "Role Conflict and Ambiguity Among School District Evaluation Unit Heads," in Bank, A., and Williams, R.C. (eds.), *Evaluation in School Districts: Organizational Perspectives*, Los Angeles: Center for the Study of Evaluation, University of California, Los Angeles, pp. 95–111.

Guba, E.G., and Lincoln, Y.S., 1981, *Effective Evaluation*, San Francisco: Jossey-Bass.

Gulick, L.H., and Urlick, L.F. (eds.), 1937, *Papers on the Science of Administration*, New York: Columbia University Press.

Guthrie, J.W. (ed.), 1980, *School Finance Policies and Practices*, Cambridge, Mass.: Ballinger.

Hall, G.E., et al., 1984, "Effects of Three Principal Studies on School Improvement," *Educational Leadership*, Vol. 41, No.5.

Hamilton, R.R., and Mort, P.R., 1941, *The Law and Public Education*, Chicago: The Foundation Press.

Hansen, E., 1979, *Educational Administration and Organizational Behavior*, Boston: Allyn and Bacon.

Harter, S., 1978, "Effectance Motivation Reconsidered," *Human Development*, Vol. 21, pp. 34–64.

Hencley, S.P., McCleary, L.E., and McGrath, 1970, *The Elementary School Principalship*, New York: Dodd, Mead.

Herman, J.J., 1973, *Developing an Effective School Staff Evaluation*, West Nyack, N.Y.: Parker.

Hertzberg, R.W., 1984, *Principals' Belief, Actions, and Accountability Regarding Student Achievement Outcomes: A Comparison of "Effective" and "Ineffective" Elementary Principals*, unpublished Ph.D. dissertation, University of California, Santa Barbara.

House, E.R., 1974, *The Politics of Educational Evaluation*, Berkeley: McCutchan.

_____, 1980, *Evaluating with Validity*, Beverly Hills: Sage.

Howsam. R.B., 1960, *Who's a Good Teacher?* Burlingame, Calif.: California School Boards Association.

Hoy, W.X., and Miskel, C.G., 1982, *Educational Administration: Theory, Research, Practice*, New York: Random House.

Iannaccone, L., 1977, "Three Views of Change in Educational Politics," in Scribner, J. (ed.), *The Politics of Education*, Chicago: The National Society for the Study of Education, pp. 255–286.

———, 1978, *Measurement in Education for the 1980s: A Politics of Education*, Santa Barbara: The Graduate School of Education, The University of California.

———, 1983, "Lessons from the 11 Nations," in Thomas, R.M. (ed.), *Politics and Education*, New York: Pergamon, Chapter 13.

Iannaccone, L., and Jangochian, R., 1985, "High Performing Curriculum and Instructional Leadership in the Climate of Excellence," *NASSP Bulletin* (May), pp. 28–35.

Immegart, G.L., and Boyd, W.L. (eds.), 1979, *Problem Finding in Educational Administration*, Lexington, Mass.: D.C. Heath.

James, H.T., 1981, "The New Cult of Efficiency and Education," in Browder, L.H. (ed.), *Emerging Patterns of Administrative Accountability*, Berkeley: McCutchan.

Janis, J.L., and Mann, L., 1977, *Decision Making*, New York: Free Press.

Johnson, G.R., 1980, *The Evaluation Component of Fiscally-Related Education Legislation*, unpublished Ph.D. dissertation, University of California, Santa Barbara.

Johnson, G.R., and Glasman, N.S., 1983, "Evaluation Authority and Financial Control: A Study of State Mandates," *Studies of Educational Evaluation*, Vol. 9, No. 1, pp. 59–76.

Joint Committee on Standards for Educational Evaluation, 1981, *Standards for Evaluations of Educational Programs, Projects, and Materials*, New York: McGraw-Hill.

Jones, H.W., 1955, *The Principal and the Principalship of Small High Schools in California*, unpublished Ph.D. dissertation, University of California, Los Angeles.

Kahneman, D., Slovic, P., and Tversky, A. (eds.), 1982, *Judgment Under Uncertainty: Heuristics and Biases*, Cambridge, Great Britain: Cambridge University Press.

Kahneman, D., and Tversky, A., 1973, "On the Psychology of Prediction," *Psychological Review*, Vol. 80, No. 4, pp. 237–251.

Kakabodes, A., and Parker, D. (eds.), 1984, *Power, Politics and Organizations*, New York: John Wiley and Sons.

Kantor, R.M., 1983, *The Change Masters*, New York: Simon and Schuster.

Katzman, M.T., 1971, *The Political Economy of Urban Schools*, Cambridge: Harvard University Press.

Kean, M.R., 1983, "Administrative Uses of Research and Evaluation Information," in Gordon, E.W. (ed.), *Review of Research in Education*, Vol. 10, pp. 361–414.

Kellaghan, T., Madaus, G.F., and Airaisian, P.W., 1982, *The Effects of Standardized Testing*, Boston: Kluer-Nijhoff.

Kelley, J., 1969, "The Study of Executive Behavior by Activity Sampling," *Human Relations*, Vol. 17, pp. 277–287.

King, J.A., and Thompson, B., 1981, *A Nationwide Survey of Administrators' Perceptions of Evaluation*, paper presented at the meeting of the American Educational Research Association, Los Angeles.

Kirp, D.L., 1982, *Just Schools*, Berkeley: University of California Press.

Klitgard, R.E., 1974, *Improving Educational Evaluation in Political Settings*, Santa Monica: The Rand Paper Series P-5327, December.

Kmetz, J.T., and Willower, D.J., 1982, "Elementary School Principals' Work Behavior," *Educational Administration Quarterly*, Vol. 18 (Fall), No. 4, pp. 62–78.

Kosekoff, J., and Fink, A., 1982, *Evaluation Basics*, Beverly Hills: Sage.

Lamb, O.L., 1961, *The Role of the Secondary Principal in the Improvement of Instruction*, unpublished Ph.D. dissertation, University of California, Los Angeles.

Landsberger, H.A., 1962, "The Horizontal Dimension of Bureaucracy," *Administrative Science Quarterly*, Vol. 6, pp. 299–332.

Langer, E.J., 1983, *The Psychology of Control*, Beverly Hills: Sage.

Lear, J., 1985, *The Evaluation Component in Administrative Decision Making: A Descriptive Study of the Use of Evaluation by Elementary School Administration*, unpublished Ph.D. dissertation, University of California, Santa Barbara.

Leithwood, K.A., and Montgomery, D.J., 1982, "The Role of the Elementary School Principal in Program Improvement," *Review of Educational Research*, Vol. 52, No. 3, pp. 309–339.

Levin, H.M., 1970, "A New Model of School Effectiveness," in Mood, A. (ed.), *Do Teachers Make a Difference?* Washington, D.C.: U.S. Department of Health, Education and Welfare, Office of Education.

Leviton, L.C., and Hughes, E.F.X., 1981, "Research on the Utilization of Evaluations; A Review of Synthesis, "*Evaluation Review*, Vol. 5, pp. 525–548.

Lewis, J., 1973, *Appraising Teacher Performance*, West Nyack, N.Y.: Parker.

Liebman, M.B., 1984, *The Use of Information Related to Student Achievement Gains in the Teacher Evaluation Process*, unpublished Ph.D. dissertation, University of California, Santa Barbara.

Light, R.J., 1979, "Capitalizing on Variation: New Conflicting Research Findings Can Be Helpful for Policy," *Educational Researcher*, Vol. 8 (October), pp. 7–11.

Likert R., 1961, *New Patterns of Management*, New York: McGraw-Hill.

Lindblom, C.E., 1959, "The Science of Muddling Through," *Public Administration Review*, Vol. 29, No. 2, pp. 79–88.

———, 1984, "Who Needs What Social Research for Policy Making?" *The Rockefeller Institute Conference Proceedings*, Vol. 1, No. 1, pp. 1–42.

Lipham, J.M., 1981, *Effective Principal, Effective School*, Reston, Va.: American Association of Secondary School Principals.

Lipham, J.M., and Hoeh, J.A. Jr., 1984, *The Principalship*, New York: Harper and Row.

Lipset, S.M., 1963, *The First New Nation: The United States in Historical and Comparative Perspective*, New York: Basic Books.

Lortie, D.C., 1975, *Schoolteacher*, Chicago: University of Chicago Press.

Lutz, F.W., and Iannaccone, L. (eds.), 1978, *Public Participation in Local School Districts*, Lexington, Mass.: Lexington.

Lyon, C.D., Dorscher, L., McGranaham, J., and Williams, R., 1978, *Evaluation and School Districts*, unpublished manuscript, Center for the Study of Evaluation. University of California, Los Angeles.

Mackenzie, D.E., 1983, "Research for School Improvement: An Appraisal of Some Recent Trends," *Educational Researcher*, Vol. 12, No. 4, pp. 5–16.

Madaus, G.F., Airasian, P.W., and Kellaghan, T., 1981, *School Effectiveness: A Reassessment of the Evidence*, New York: McGraw-Hill.

Madden, J.V., et al., 1978, *School Effectiveness Study: State of California*, Sacramento, Calif.: State of California Department of Education.

March, J.G., (ed.), 1965, *Handbook of Organizations*, Chicago: Rand McNally.

Margalith, A., 1980, *Decisions and Consequences in Israeli Secondary Education*, unpublished Ph.D. dissertation, University of California, Santa Barbara.

McAbee, H.V., 1958, "Time for the Job," *NASSP Bulletin*, Vol. 42, pp. 39–44.

McCarthy, D.P., Lazarus, A., and Canner, J., 1980, *School Improvement Project: A Summary of the First Annual Assessment Report*, New York: Office of Educational Evaluation, New York City Public Schools.

McGregor, D., 1973, *The Human Side of the Enterprise*, New York: Harper and Row.

McLaughlin, M.W., 1984, *Implementation Realities and Evaluation Design*, Stanford, Calif.: Stanford University, Institute for Research of Educational Finance and Governance, #84-B1.

Michelsen, S., 1970, "The Association of the Teacher Resources with Children's Characteristics," in Mood, A. (ed.), *Do Teachers Make a Difference?* Washington, D.C.: U.S. Department of Health, Education and Welfare, Office of Education.

Millman, J. (ed.), 1981, *Handbook of Teacher Evaluation*, Beverly Hills: Sage.

Mintzberg, H., 1973, *The Nature of Managerial Work*, New York: Harper and Row.

Mitchell, D.E., Ortiz, F.I., and Mitchell, T.K., 1984, "What is the Incentive to Teach?", *Politics of Education Bulletin*, Vol. 11 (Spring) No. 2, pp. 1–6, 11.

Mitchell, D.E., and Spady, W.G., 1978, "Organizational Contexts for Implementing Outcome Based Education," *Educational Researcher*, Vol. 7 (July/August), pp. 9–17.

Molitor, L. Th., Jr., 1981, *Size and Substance of the Evaluation Component in High School Administration*, unpublished Ph.D. dissertation, University of California, Santa Barbara.

Moore, M.T., 1975, *The Boundary-Spanning Role of the Urban High School Principal*, unpublished Ph.D. dissertation, University of California, Los Angeles.

Morris, V.C., Crowson, R.L., Hurwitz, E., and Porter-Gehrie, C., 1981, *The Urban Principalship*, Chicago: University of Chicago Press.

Mort, P.R., 1946, *Principals of School Administration*, New York: McGraw-Hill.

Mort, P.R., Rensger, W.C., and Polley, J.W., 1960, *Public School Finance*, New York: McGraw-Hill.

Mosteller, F., and Moynihan, D.P. (eds.), 1972, *On Equality of Educational Opportunity*, New York: Vintage.

Murnane, R.J., 1975, *The Impact of School Resources on the Learning of Inner City Children*, Cambridge, Mass.: Ballinger.

Nagel, S.S. (ed.), 1980, *Improving Policy Analysis*, Beverly Hills: Sage.

Natriello, G., and Dornbusch, S.N., 1980–81, "Pitfalls in the Evaluation of Teachers by Principals," *Administrator's Notebook*, Vol. 29, No. 6, pp. 1–4.

Nevo, D., 1983, "The Conceptualization of Educational Evaluation: An Analytical Review of the Literature," *Review of Educational Research*, Vol. 53 (Spring), No. 1, pp. 117–128.

Niedermeyer, F., and Klein, S, 1972, "An Empirical Evaluation of a District Teachers Accountability Program," *Phi Delta Kappan*, Vol. 54, No.2, pp. 100–103.

Olivero, J.L., 1980, *The Principalship in California*, Burlingame, Calif.: The Association of California School Administrators.

O'Reilly, C., 1981, "Evaluation Information and Decision Making in Organizations," in Bank, A., and Williams, R.C. (eds.), *Evaluation in School Districts: Organizational Perspectives*, Los Angeles: Center for the Study of Evaluation, University of California, Los Angeles, pp. 25–64.

Ouchi, W.G., 1980, "Markets, Bureaucracies, and Clans," *Administrative Science Quarterly*, Vol. 25, No. 1, pp. 129–141.

Patterson, B.B., 1984, *Perceptions of Efficacy in Effective and Ineffective Principals*, unpublished Ph.D. dissertation, University of California, Santa Barbara.

Patton, M.Q., 1978, *Utilization-Focused Evaluation*, Beverly Hills: Sage.

———, 1980, *Qualitative Evaluation Methods*, Beverly Hills: Sage.

———, 1982, *Practical Evaluation*, Beverly Hills: Sage.

Paulin, P.J., 1980, *The Influence of Teacher Autonomy on Resistance to Evaluation*, unpublished Ph.D. dissertation, University of California, Santa Barbara.

Perrow, C., 1965, "Hospitals: Technology, Structure and Goals," in March, J.G. (ed.), *Handbook of Organizations*, Chicago: Rand McNally.

Peters, T.J., and Waterman, R.H., 1982, *In Search for Excellence*, New York: Harper and Row.

Phi Delta Kappa, 1980, *Why Do Some Urban Schools Succeed?* Bloomington, Ind.: Phi Delta Kappa and Indiana University Press.

Pohland, P., and Cross, J., 1981, "Impact of the Curriculum on Supervision," in Sergiovanni, T.J. (ed.), *Supervision of Teaching*, Alexandria, Va.: Association of Supervision and Curriculum Development.

Popham, W.J., 1971, *Designing Teacher Evaluation Systems*, Los Angeles: The Instructional Objectives Exchange.

Powell, M., and Beard, J.W., 1984, *Teacher Effectiveness*, New York: Garland.

Provus, M.M., 1967, *Big City Title I Evaluation Conference*, Pittsburgh: Pittsburgh Public Schools.

Purkey, S.C., and Smith, M.S., 1983, "Effective Schools: A Review," *The Elementary School Journal*, Vol. 83, No. 4, pp. 427–452.

Reeder, W.G., 1951, *The Fundamentals of Public School Administration*, New York: MacMillan.

Rein, M., and White, S.H., 1977, "Can Policy Research Help Policy?" *The Public Interest*, Vol. 49 (Fall), pp. 119–136.

Rich, R.E., 1981, *Social Science Information and Public Policy*, San Francisco: Jossey-Bass.

Roe, W., and Drake, T., 1980, *The Principalship*, New York: MacMillan.

Rogers, V., Talbot, C., and Cosgrove, E., 1984, "Excellence," *Educational Leadership*, February, pp. 39–41.

Rosenholz, S.J., and Wilson, B., 1980, "The Effect of Classroom Structure on Shared Perceptions of Ability," *American Educational Research Journal*, Vol. 17, pp. 75–82.

Rotter, J., 1975, "Some Problems and Misconceptions Related to the Construct of Internal Versus External Control of Reinforcement," *Journal of Consulting and Clinical Psychology*, Vol. 43, pp. 56–68.

Russell, J., and Mazzarella, J.A., 1984, "Linking the Behaviors and Activities of Secondary School Principals to School Effectiveness," Eugene, Oreg.: Center for Educational Policy and Management, University of Oregon.

Rutherford, W.L., and Hoffman, J.V., 1981, "Toward Implementation of the ESEA Title I Evaluation and Reporting System: A Concerns Analysis," *Educational Evaluation and Policy Analysis*, Vol. 3, No. 4, pp. 17–23.

Rutter, N., et al., 1979, *Fifteen Thousand Hours*, Cambridge: Harvard University Press.

Ryan, W., 1981, *Equality*, New York: Random House.

Sarason, S., 1982, *The Culture of the School and the Problem of Change*, Boston: Allyn and Bacon.

Sax, G., 1974, "The Use of Standardized Tests in Evaluation," in Popham, W.J. (ed.), *Evaluation in Education*, Berkeley: McCutchan, Chapter 5.

Scribner, J.D. (ed.), 1977, *The Politics of Education*, Chicago: The University of Chicago Press.

Scriven, M., 1967, "The Methodology of Evaluation," in Stake, R.E. (ed.), *AERA Monograph Series on Curriculum Evaluation*, Chicago: Rand McNally, No. 1.

———, 1973, "Goal Free Evaluation," in House, E.R. (ed.), *School Evaluation: The Political Process*, Berkeley: McCutchan.

Seligman, M., 1975, *Helplessness: Effects on Depression, Development, and Death*. San Francisco: Freeman.

Sergiovanni, T.J., 1982, "Ten Principles for Quality Leadership," *Educational Leadership*, Vol. 39, No. 5, pp. 330–336.

———, 1984, "Leadership and Excellence in Schooling," *Education Leadership*, February, 4–13.

Shapiro, M., 1980, *Federal Regulation of Education*, Stanford, Calif.: Institute for Research on Educational Finance and Governance, Stanford University, Report No. 80-B17.

Shavelson, R., and Dempsy-Atwood, N., 1976, "Generalizability of Measures of Teaching Behavior," *Review of Educational Research*, Vol. 46, No. 4, pp. 553–611.

Shoemaker, J., and Fraser, H.W., 1981, "What Principals Can Do: Some Implications from Studies of Effective Schooling," *Phi Delta Kappan* (November), pp. 178–182.

Simon, H.A., 1975, *Administrative Behavior*, New York: Macmillan.

———, 1960, *The New Science of Management Decision*, New York: Harper and Row.

Smith, N.L., 1982, *Communication Strategies in Evaluation*, Beverly Hills: Sage.

Smith, S.C., Mazzarella, J.A., and Piele, P.K. (eds.), 1981, *School Leadership*, Eugene, Oreg.: Clearinghouse on Educational Management, University of Oregon.

Sproull, L., 1977, *Managerial Attention in New Education Programs: A Micro-Behavioral Study of Program Implementation*, unpublished Ph.D. dissertation, Stanford University, Stanford, California.

Sproull, L.S., 1979, *Response to Regulation: An Organizational Process Framework*, Pittsburgh: Carnegie Mellon University.

Sproull, L., 1981, "Managerial Attention," *Human Organization*, Vol. 40, pp. 114–122.

Srivastra, S. (ed.), 1983, *The Executive Mind*, San Francisco,: Jossey-Bass.

Sroufe, G.E., 1977, "Evaluation and Politics," in Scribner, J.D. (ed.), *The Politics of Education*, Chicago: University of Chicago Press.

Stake, R.E., 1967, "The Countenance of Educational Evaluation," *Teachers College Record*, Vol. 68, pp. 523–540.

Stallings, J., 1980, "Allocated Academic Learning Time Revisited," *Educational Researcher*, Vol. 9, pp. 11–16.

State of New York, Office of Performance Review, 1974, *School Factors Influencing Reading Achievement: A Case Study of Two Inner City Schools*, Albany, N.Y.

Stecher, B.B., Alkin, M.C., and Flesher, G., 1981, *Patterns of Information Use in School Level Decision Making*, Los Angeles: Center for the Study of Evaluation, University of California, Los Angeles.

Stipek, D.J., and Weiss, J.R., 1981, "Perceived Personal Control and Academic Achievement," *Review of Educational Research*, Vol. 51, No. 1, pp. 101–137.

Stow, S.B., 1979, "Using Effectiveness Research in Teacher Evaluation," *Educational Leadership*, Vol. 37, No. 1, pp. 55–58.

Stufflebeam, D.L., 1966, "A Depth Study of the Evaluation Requirement," *Theory Into Practice*, Vol. 5 (June), pp. 121–134.

———, 1974a, *Meta-Evaluation*, Kalamazoo, Mich.: Center for Evaluation, Western Michigan University, Occasional Paper No. 3, December.

————, 1974b, "Alternative Approaches to Educational Evaluation: A Self Study Guide for Educators," in Popham, W.J. (ed.), *Evaluation in Education*, Berkeley: McCutchan, pp. 95–144.

————, 1985, "Coping With the Point of Entry Problems in Evaluating Projects," *Studies in Educational Evaluation*, Vol. 11, No. 2, pp. 123–130.

Stufflebeam, D.L., et al., 1971, *Educational Evaluation and Decision Making*, Itasca, Ill.: F.E. Peacock.

Suchman, E.A., 1967, *Evaluative Research*, New York: Russel Sage Foundation.

Sweeney, J., 1982, "Research Synthesis on Effective School Leadership," *Educational Leadership* (February), pp. 346–352.

Taylor, F.W., 1911, *Shop Management*, New York: Harper and Row.

Taylor, K.M., and Betz, N.E., 1983, "Applications of Self-Efficacy Theory to the Understanding and Treatment of Career Indecision," *Journal of Vocational Behavior*, Vol. 22, pp. 63–81.

Thomas, M.D., 1979, "Performance Evaluation of Educational Personnel," ERIC ED 179 204.

Thompson, M.S., 1982, *Decision Analysis for Program Evaluation*, Cambridge, Mass.: Ballinger.

Triplett, J.W., 1961, *A Functional Analysis of Elementary School Principals*, unpublished Ph.D. dissertation, University of California, Los Angeles.

Tsang, M., and Levin, H.M., 1983, "The Impact of Intergovernmental Grants on Educational Expenditure," *Review of Educational Research*, Vol. 53, No. 3, pp. 329–368.

Tuckman, B.W., 1979, *Evaluating Instructional Programs*, Boston: Allyn and Bacon.

Tyack, D., and Hansot, E., 1982, *Managers of Virtue: Public School Leadership in America, 1820–1980*, New York: Basic Books.

Tyler, R.W., 1950, *Basic Principles of Curriculum and Evaluation*, Chicago: University of Chicago Press.

United States Department of Education, 1984, *The Nation Responds: Recent Efforts to Improve Education*, Washington, D.C.: U.S. Government Printing Office.

Venezky, R.L., and Winfield, L.F., 1979, *Schools That Succeed Beyond Expectations in Reading*, Newark, Del.: Studies in Education, Technical Report No. 1.

Vial, J.N., *Student Achievement Data-Based Program Evaluation: A Concern for Principals*, unpublished Ph.D. dissertation, University of California, Santa Barbara.

Vroom, V.H., 1976, "Can Leaders Learn to Lead?" *Organizational Dynamics*, Vol. 3, pp. 17–28.

Vroom, V.H., and Yago, A.G., 1974, "Decisionmaking as a Social Process: Normative and Descriptive Models of Leader Behavior," *Decision Sciences*, Vol. 5, pp. 743–768.

Vroom, V.H., and Yetton, P.W., 1973, *Leadership and Decision Making*. Pittsburgh: University of Pittsburgh Press.

Walberg, H.J. (ed.), 1982, *Improving Educational Standards and Productivity: The Research Basis for Policy*, Berkeley: McCutchan.

Weber, G., 1971, *Inner-City Children Can Be Taught To Read: Four Successful Schools*, Washington, D.C.: Council for Basic Education.

Webster, W., and Stufflebeam, D., 1978, *The State of Theory and Practice in Educational Evaluation in Large Urban School Districts*, paper presented at the meeting of the American Educational Research Association, Toronto, Canada.

Weick, K.E., 1968, "Systematic Observational Method," in Lindzey, G., and Aronson, E.A. (eds.), *The Handbook of Social Psychology*, Reading, Mass.: Addison, Wesley.

———, 1976, "Educational Organizations as Loosely Coupled Systems," *Administrative Science Quarterly*, Vol. 21, pp. 1–19.

———, 1982, "Administering Education in Loosely Coupled Schools," *Phi Delta Kappan*, Vol. 63, No. 10, pp. 673–676.

Weiner, B., 1980, *Human Motivation*. New York: Holt, Rinehart and Winston.

Weiss, C.H., 1980, "Measuring the Use of Evaluation," in Ciarlo, J.A. (ed.), *Utilizing Evaluation: Concepts and Measurement Techniques*, Beverly Hills: Sage.

———, 1981, "An EEPA Interview with Carol H. Weiss," *Educational Evaluation and Policy Analysis*, Vol. 2, No. 5, pp. 75–79.

Weldy, G.A., 1974, *Time: A Resource for the School Administrator*, Reston, Va.: National Association of Secondary School Principals.

Wellisch, J.B., et al., 1978 "School Management and Organization in Successful Schools," *Sociology of Education*, Vol. 51 (July), pp. 211–226.

Wildavsky, A., 1972, "The Self-Evaluating Organization," *Public Administration Review*. Vol. 32, No. 5, pp. 82–93.

Wiles, D.K., Wiles, J., and Bondi, J., 1981, *Practical Politics for School Administration*, Boston: Allyn and Bacon.

Willis, Q., 1980, "The Work Activity of School Principals: An Observational Study," *The Journal of Educational Administration*, Vol. 18, No. 1, pp. 27–54.

Winkler, D.R., 1979, "Fiscal Limitations in the Provision of Local Public Services: The Case of Education," *National Tax Journal*, Vol. 32, No. 2, pp. 329–342.

Wirt, F.M., 1978, *Does Control Follow the Dollar? Value Analysis, School Policy and State-Local Linkages*, New York: American Political Science Association.

Wirt, F.M., and Kirst, M.W., 1982, *Schools in Conflict*, Berkeley: McCutchan.

Wolcott, H., 1973, *The Man in the Principal's Office*, New York: Holt, Rinehart and Winston.

Wynne, E., 1972, *The Politics of School Accountability*, Berkeley: McCutchan.

Zak, I., and Glasman, N.S., 1979, "State Aid, Voter Power and Local Control in Education," *National Tax Journal*, Vol. 32, No. 2, pp. 371–373.

Ziegler, L.H., Tucker, H.J., and Wilson, L.A., 1977, "How School Control Was Wrested from the People," *Phi Delta Kappan*, Vol. 58, No. 7, pp. 534–539.

Zucker, L.G., 1981, "Institutional Structure and Organizational Processes: The Role of Evaluation Unit in Schools" in Bank, A., and Williams, R.C. (eds.), *Evaluation in School Districts: Organizational Perspectives*, Los Angeles: Center for the Study of Evaluation, University of California, Los Angeles, pp. 69–89.

Index

Accountability
  criteria of, 24–25
  demands for, 23–26, 46, 83, 85, 90, 163
  effectiveness and, 116
  financial, 25
  of teachers, 73, 75–77, 164
  principals and, 74–77, 117
Airaisian, P. W., 54, 64
Alkin, M. C., 10, 14, 25, 39, 41, 48, 64
Andersen, R. H., 64
Argyris, C., 58

Baker, E. L., 64
Bandura, A., 171
Bank, A., 34, 38, 41, 49
Barnard, C., 24
Beard, J. W., 12
Berk, R. A., 13, 22
Berman, P., 106
Betz, N. E., 171
Bickel, W. E., 39–40
Bidwell, C. E., 12, 64, 170
Bilazewski, B. V., 49, 124–125
Biniaminov, I., 54
Bloom, B. S., 25
Bolman, L. G., 166
Bondi, J., 47
Bossert, S., 53
Boyd, W. L., 20

Brewer, E., 135
Brickell, H. M., 22
Bridge, R. G., 54, 64
Bridges, E. M., 46
Brookover, W. B., 56, 65, 106
Brown, R. D., 65, 171
Bruner, J., 167
Burns, T., 135
Burry, J., 34, 38, 41, 49, 171

Calfee, R., 65
California State Department of Education, 106
Callahan, R. E., 22, 24, 46
Campbell, R. F., 22, 30
Canner, J., 56
Carlson, S., 135
Centra, J. A., 54
Coats, W. D., 64
Cohen, D. K., 20
Cohen, M., 56, 64
Cohn, E., 54
Coleman, J. S., 25, 64
Control
  funding and, 4, Chapter 3
  perceptions of, 58, 116
Cooley, W. W., 39–40
Corbally, J. E., Jr., 22
Cosgrove, E., 160
Cronbach, L. J., 10–11, 44
Cross, J., 64

Crowson, R. L., xv
Cuban, L., 34
Cubberly, E. P., 22
Cunningham, L. L., 30, 46
Cuttitta, F. F., 126

Daillak, R. H., 14, 39, 48
Deal, T., xv, 116
de Charmes, R., 171
Deci, E., 171
Dempsy-Atwood, N., 12
Dillman, D. A., 68
Dornbusch, S. M., 16, 59, 171
Dornhoff, G. W., 23
Dorr-Bremme, D., 61, 100
Dorscher, L., 39
Drake, T., 46
Dubin, 135
Duckworth, K., 64, 171
Duignan, P., 135
Duke, D. L., xv, 43, 57

Easton, D., 19
Ebel, R. L., 64
Edmonds, R. R., 56, 64
Educational policy, 19–21, 24, 26
Educational value conflicts, 21–23, 26
Effective schools research, 55–57, 61,
  65
Effectiveness
  of principals, 56–57, 66, 68, 116, 171
  of schools, 40, 56–57, 61, 64
Eisner, E. W., 11–12
Ellis, A. B., 57
Evaluation
  activities, 128–130, 149–150
  and finance, 28–32
  as measurement behavior, 9–12
  decision making and, 10–11, 14, 59,
    115, 123–124, 131, 133–134,
    136–139, 142, 145–146, 148–151,
    154–156, 164–166, 169–172
  definitions of, 1–2, 9–11, 16, 44,
    123–124, 126, 141–142, 151
  demands for, 2–3, 5, 49, 163
  history of, 9–15

mandates, 27, 34, 48–49, 83, 95, 105,
  115
methods, 9, 13–14, 16, 37, 40, 49
models, 15–17, 123–125, 131, 134,
  141–143, 154, 158–160
  of curriculum 10, 48
  of instructional objectives, 10, 63
  of programs, 14–15, 44, 48, 63,
    Chapter 9, 115–117
  of student achievement, 12–13, 35, 44,
    48, 58, 63, 83, 105–107, 119
  of teachers, 12, 35, 43, 48, 64, 76,
    Chapter 10, 115–116, 164
orientation, 45–47, 124–125
purposes, 28–29, 36–38, 44, 46, 115,
  119, 121, 123–124, 127–131, 133,
  158
reported time engaged in, 126–127,
128–131
standards, 15
subjectivity in, 12–13, 49, 169
systematized, 27, 33–34, 38, 40–41,
  45, 47, 172
uses of, information, 14, 38, 40,
  Chapters 9–10, 115–116, 118–119,
  123–124, 164

Federal Government, 27–30, 47–48
Fielder, F. E., 135
Fink, A., 48
Firestone, W. A., xv
Flanders, N. A., 12
Flesher, G., 48
Friedericksen, J. R., 56
Fuller, B., 171

Gally, J., 133–135, 138–139, 141–143,
  147, 149
Garms, W. I., 23
Gephart, W. J., 46
Glaser, R., 12
Glasman, N. S., 2, 11–12, 16, 21,
  24–25, 28–32, 34, 38, 48–49, 53–54,
  62, 96, 123–125, 142–143, 171
Glass, G. V., 11–12, 20, 64
Goldhammer, R., 64

Gorton, R. A., 126
Granger, R. L., 46
Griffiths, D. E., 111, 123, 156, 159
Grunsky, O., 36
Guba, E. G., 11
Gulick, E. G., 135
Guthrie, J. W., 23

Hack, W. G., 30
Hall, G. E., 56
Hamilton, R. R., 44
Hansen, E., 170
Hansot, E., 46
Hartner, S., 171
Hencley, S. P., 46
Herman, J. J., 64
Hertzberg, R. W., 63
Hoeh, J. A., Jr., 46, 126
Hoffman, J. V., 28, 56
House, E. R., 11, 44
Howsam, R. B., 64
Hoy, W. X., 63
Hughes, E. F. X., 39
Hurwitz, E., xv

Iannaccone, L., xv, 21-22, 30
Imber, M., 57
Immegart, G. L., 20
Information
  awareness of, 123, 142, 146-147, 155
  exchange of, 139, 141-142, 147,
    149-150, 154-156, 165-166
  for decision making, 126, 131, 133,
    139, 147, 154, 166
  judgment of the worth of, 1, 59, 90,
    123, 126, 139, 142, 145-147,
    149-150, 154-155, 157, 159, 166
  sources of, 154

James, H. T., 24
Jamgochian, R., xv
Janis, J. L., 171
Johnson, G. R., 16, 28
Joint Committee on Standards for
  Educational Evaluation, 15, 44
Jones, H. W., 126

Judd, C. M., 54, 64
Judgment
  intentionality in, 126, 139, 166
  rendering of, 5, 49, 123, 139,
    154-156, 158, 166-167, 169
  subjective: See Subjectivity in
  decision making.
Judgmental component, 5, 139, 153,
  156-160, 166

Kahneman, D., 2, 167
Kakabodes, A., xv
Kantor, R. M., xv
Kasarda, J., 64, 170
Katzman, M. T., 54
Kean, M. R., 171
Kellaghan, T., 54, 64
Kelley, J., 135
Kennedy, A., xv
King, J. A., 39
Kirp, D. L., 25
Kirst, M. W., 19
Klaus, D. J., 12
Klein, S., 64
Klitgard, R. E., 20
Kmetz, J. T., 63
Kosekoff, J., 48
Krajewski, R. J., 64

Lamb, O. L., 126
Landsberger, H. A., 135
Langer, E. J., 58, 171
Lazarus, A., 56
Lear, J., 141-143, 146-147, 149
Leithwood, K. A., 53, 106
Levin, H. M., 29, 54
Leviton, L. C., 39
Lewis, J., 64
Liebman, M. B., 64
Light, R. J., 20
Likert, R., 135
Lincoln, Y. S., 11
Lindblom, C. E., 3, 135
Lipham, J. M., 46, 126
Lipset, S. M., 25

Local government, 30
Lortie, D. C., 64
Lutz, F. W., 22, 30
Lyon, C. D., 39

Mackenzie, D. E., 56
Madaus, G. F., 54, 64
Madden, J. V., 56
Mann, L., 171
March, J. G., 64, 135
Mazzarella, J. A., xv, 46
McAbee, H. V., 126
McCarthy, D. P., 56
McCleary, L. E., 46
McGranaham, J., 39
McGrath, 46
McLaughlin, M. W., 106, 125
Michelsen, S., 54
Millman, J., 12, 64
Millman, S. D., 54
Mintzberg, H., 135
Miskel, C. E., 63
Mitchell, D. E., 63–64, 159
Mitchell, T. K., 159
Molitar, L. T., Jr., 123, 125–126, 131, 133, 142
Montgomery, D. J., 53, 106
Moock, P. R., 54, 64
Moore, M. T., 126
Morris, V. C., xv
Mort, P. R., 22, 44
Mosteller, F., 25
Moynihan, D. P., 25
Murnane, R. J., 54

Nagel, S. S., 23
Natriello, G., 59
Nevo, D., 17, 44, 142
Newman, D. L., 171
Niedermeyer, F., 64
Nystrand, R. O., 30

Olivero, J. L., 46, 65
Olsen, J. P., 64
O'Reilly, C., 41, 63

Organizations
    evaluation and, 27–32, 38–39, 43, 45, 166–167
Ortiz, F. I., 159
Ouchi, W. G., 59

Patterson, B. B., 111
Patton, M. Q., 13, 15, 48
Parker, D., xv
Paulin, P. J., 48, 96
Perrow, C., 39
Peters, T. J., xv, 159
Phi Delta Kappa, 57
Piele, P. K., 46
Pierce, L. C., 23
Pohland, P., 64
Polley, J. W., 22, 44
Popham, W. J., 64
Porter-Gehrie, C., xv
Potter, D. A., 54
Powell, M., 12
Provus, M. M., 10
Purkey, S. C., 64

Quellmalz, E. S., 64

Ramseyer, J. A., 22
Rapoport, T., 171
Reeder, W. G., 43
Rein, M., 20
Rich, R. E., 39
Rivers, L. S., 171
Roe, W., 46
Rogers, V., 160
Rosenholz, S. J., 65
Rossi, P. H., 22
Rotter, J., 171
Russell, J., xv
Ruskus, J., 41
Rutherford, W. L., 28, 56
Ryan, W., 25

Sax, G., 25
School Administration, 30, 123, 159
School Districts

decision making patterns of, 33–34,
36–39, 45
history of, 33
management of, 33–37
policies in, 33, 35, 37
regulation of funds given to, 31–32
structure of, 33, 35–38
use of evaluation in, 36–41
School leadership, 1, 3, 56, 64–65, 77,
83, 105, 111, 123–125, 131, 133,
153, 156, 163–166, 169, 172
and evaluator role, 43–48, 123–124,
165
School principals
as decision makers, 47, 123–124,
126–127, 131, 133–134, 136–139,
141–142, 145–146, 148–152,
164–165, 170
as evaluators, 3, 5, 46–49, 84–85, 96,
103, 115–118, 121, 123, 125–131,
163–165
as leaders, 54
attributes of, and student achievement,
53–56
demands on 2, 3, 5
elementary, 61, 65, 125, 141, 147,
149, 154–155, 157, 159, 163, 166
involvement of, in solving student
achievement problems, Chapter 11
secondary, 65, 125, 131, 135, 149,
154, 157, 159, 163, 165
Scott, W. R., 16
Scribner, J. D., 19
Scriven, M., 11–12, 48
Seligman, M., 171
Sell, R., 2, 123, 142
Sergiovanni, T. J., 64, 160
Shapiro, M., 32
Shavelson, R., 12
Simon, A., 12
Simon, H. A., 135, 167
Slovic, P., 167
Smith, M. S., 64
Smith, N. L., 48
Smith, S. C., 46

Spady, W. G., 63–64
Sproull, L., 59, 135
Sprya, S. L., 135
Srivastra, S., 160
Sroufe, G. E., 22
Stake, R. E., 11
Stallings, J., 65
State Government, 27, 29–30, 47
State of New York, Office of
Performance Review, 56–57
Stecher, B. B., 48
Stipek, D. J., 171
Stow, S. B., 64
Student achievement
determinants of, 55–57, 59
influence of principal on, 53–55, 57,
68, 72, 113–119
problems with, 53, 64, 105–111,
118–119
sharing of data on, 95–100, 103, 114
use of, data by principals, 61–65, 68,
72, 75, 115–117, Chapter 9,
Chapter 10, 114–116, 119, 152,
163–164
Stufflebeam, D. L., 10–11, 36–40, 48,
123, 134, 138, 141, 154–155
Subjectivity in decision making, 11–13,
49, 166, 169
Suchman, E. A., 142
Sweeney, J., 64

Talbot, C., 160
Taylor, F. W., 24
Taylor, K. M., 171
Thomas, M. D., 64
Thompson, B., 39
Thompson, M. S., 2
Tomlinson, J. W., 135
Triplett, J. W., 126
Tsang, M., 29
Tucker, H. J., 22
Tuckman, B. W., 15
Tversky, A., 21, 167
Tyack, D., 46
Tyler, R. W., 10, 25

United States Department of Education, 23

University of California, Santa Barbara, 34, 38, 61–62, 66, 121, 125, 170–171

Urlick, L. F., 135

Usdan, M. D., 30

Venezky, R. L., 106

Vroom, V. H., 171

Walberg, H. J., 54

Weber, G., 56

Webster, W., 39

Weick, K. E., 58, 64, 135

Weiner, B., 171

Weiss, C. H., 39

Weiss, J. A., 20

Weiss, J. R., 171

Weldy, G. A., 126

Wellisch, J. B., 57, 65, 106

White, P., 14, 39, 48

White, S. H., 20

Wildavsky, A., 27

Wiles, D. K., 47

Wiles, J., 47

Williams, R. C., 34, 38

Willower, D. J., 63

Wilson, B. L., xv, 65

Wilson, L. A., 22

Winfield, L. F., 106

Winkler, D. R., 31

Wirt, F. M., 19, 30

Wolcott, H., 46, 126, 135, 143

Wood, K., 171

Wynne, E., 25

Yago, A. G., 171

Zak, I., 30

Ziegler, L. H., 22

Zucker, L. G., 36, 40